P9-EMH-241

Don't Give In...
God Wants
YOU
to Win!

THELMA WELLS

HARVEST HOUSE PUBLISHERS

EUGENE, OREGON

Unless otherwise indicated, Scripture quotations are taken from the New King James Version. Copyright © 1982 by Thomas Nelson, Inc. Used by permission. All rights reserved.

Verses marked NASB: New American Standard Bible®, © 1960, 1962, 1963, 1968, 1971, 1972, 1973, 1975, 1977, 1995 by The Lockman Foundation. Used by permission. (www.Lockman.org)

Verses marked NLT: Holy Bible, New Living Translation, copyright © 1996, 2004. Used by permission of Tyndale House Publishers, Inc., Wheaton, IL 60189 USA. All rights reserved.

Verses marked ESV: Holy Bible, English Standard Version, copyright © 2001 by Crossway Bibles, a division of Good News Publishers. Used by permission. All rights reserved.

Verses marked MSG: The Message. Copyright © by Eugene H. Peterson 1993, 1994, 1995, 1996, 2000, 2001, 2002. Used by permission of NavPress Publishing Group.

Verses marked PHILLIPS: J.B. Phillips: The New Testament in Modern English, Revised Edition. © J.B. Phillips 1958, 1960, 1972. Used by permission of Macmillan Publishing.

Verses marked KJV: King James Version of the Bible.

Verses marked NIV: HOLY BIBLE, NEW INTERNATIONAL VERSION®. NIV®. Copyright © 1973, 1978, 1984 by the International Bible Society. Used by permission of Zondervan. All rights reserved.

Verses marked TLB: The Living Bible, Copyright © 1971. Used by permission of Tyndale House Publishers, Inc., Wheaton, IL 60189 USA. All rights reserved.

Harvest House Publishers has made every effort to trace the ownership of all quotes. In the event of a question arising from the use of a quote, we regret any error made and will be pleased to make the necessary correction in future editions of this book.

Italics in Scripture quotations indicate author's emphasis.

Published in association with Van Diest Literary Agency, PO Box 1482, Sisters, OR 97759.

Back cover photo: Shooting Starr Photography—by Cindi Starr, www.shootingstarrphotos.com

Cover by Abris, Veneta, Oregon

DON'T GIVE IN—GOD WANTS YOU TO WIN!
Copyright © 2009 by Thelma Wells
Published by Harvest House Publishers
Eugene, Oregon 97402
www.harvesthousepublishers.com

Library of Congress Cataloging-in-Publication Data

Wells, Thelma.
Don't give in—God wants you to win! / Thelma Wells.
     p. cm.
Includes bibliographical references.
ISBN 978-0-7369-2614-0 (pbk.)
1. Spiritual warfare. 2. Christian life. I. Title.
BV4509.5.W398 2009
248.8'6—dc22   2008035419

All rights reserved. No part of this publication may be reproduced, stored in a retrieval system, or transmitted in any form or by any means—electronic, mechanical, digital, photocopy, recording, or any other—except for brief quotations in printed reviews, without the prior permission of the publisher.

Printed in the United States of America

09 10 11 12 13 14 15 16 17 / VP-KB / 10 9 8 7 6 5 4 3 2 1

Hear ye, hear ye! All people of the world who have issues, situations, circumstances, and problems—

Are you sick and tired of being sick and tired? I am! Discover how to handle difficulties, ways to protect yourself, and strategies for winning. We'll also explore how to get the most joy out of life.

I dedicate this book to you with the hope and prayer that it will help you fight the good fight of faith and win every battle against the wiles of the devil.

You deserve a break—today, tomorrow, and forever. You deserve freedom in your life. You deserve peace of mind. You deserve contentment. You deserve righteousness. You deserve to know how to fight and win. Every word in this book is designed to help you attain those goals.

You deserve to know how to win over the enemy! Are you ready? Let's get started!

Contents

The Way to Victory

James Robison

Thelma Wells understands what too few Christians comprehend: The real battle affecting everything in our lives is waged in the invisible realm. The spiritual influences and impact of the realm of darkness and deception not only distract believers, but lead them far too often into recurring defeat.

Old Testament prophet Jeremiah clearly emphasized that God's chosen people are led away captive by the adversary. Isaiah said the tormentors influence you to lie down and become a smooth road for them to trample on (see Isaiah 51:23). Visit a typical church and you'll see people marching in and out as though they are held hostage or, in some instances, appear to be in a chain gang. Where is the freedom?

Solomon said we are often bound by the cords of our own iniquity. Our weaknesses and sinful tendencies are points of obvious vulnerability where the enemy fiercely attacks. Satan has in his grasp the lives of all unbelievers because, as Jesus said, they are of our father, the devil (John 8:44), and Paul said they are by nature the children of wrath (Ephesians 2:3). Thus, the enemy is focusing his fiercest attack not against the unbeliever already by nature doing his will, but rather on the host of believers—on Christians. Because we're often unaware of this reality, many Christians don't understand that their thoughts are often not their own. They are suggestions of the enemy. When these thoughts and feelings of hurt, bitterness, or lust take root, they become flaming arrows. People often burn with such thoughts and feelings.

Many believers are suffering because of unfortunate circumstances in their childhoods. Because these wounds have never healed, the people are continually downtrodden. Some Old Testament prophets use the illustration of birds of prey attacking the vulnerable sheep. Wolves also always attack the most vulnerable in the flock. A careful reading of the book of Lamentations will reveal what Thelma has come to know, and what all believers must see: When God's people are continually defeated, we must understand what most people even in the Old Testament didn't believe: The enemy does in fact enter the gates of Jerusalem to destroy the splendor of God.

Satan is an accuser of the brethren. He will turn family member against family member. Every foul, tormenting spirit of harlotry, bitterness, anger, and idolatry (which includes some religious traditions) is having far too great an effect in the lives of professing Christians.

Thelma has discovered the reality of this battle, but she's also found the way to victory. Through all the trials and testing of our faith, we can grow in the grace and knowledge of our Lord and truly become "more than conquerors in Christ." As Scripture proclaims, "Greater is He that is in us than He that is in the world!" (1 John 4:4). Through His power—and only through His power—we can overcome the enemy. We need the wisdom of God, the power of the Holy Spirit, and the encouragement of our fellow believers. Thelma inspires us all to find the help and hope that come only through the sufficiency of our Lord Jesus. She is a friend of Betty and my ministry, LIFE Outreach, and she is a blessing to the body of Christ.

James Robison
Founder and president,
LIFE Outreach International
Fort Worth, Texas

Finally, my brethren, be strong in the Lord
and in the power of His might.
Put on the whole armor of God, that you may be able
to stand against the wiles of the devil.
For we do not wrestle against flesh and blood,
but against principalities, against powers, against the rulers
of the darkness of this age, against spiritual hosts of wickedness
in the heavenly places.
Therefore take up the whole armor of God,
that you may be able to withstand
in the evil day, and having done all, to stand.

Stand therefore, having girded your waist with truth,
having put on the breastplate of righteousness,
and having shod your feet with the preparation
of the gospel of peace;
above all, taking the shield of faith with which you will
be able to quench all the fiery darts of the wicked one.
And take the helmet of salvation,
and the sword of the Spirit, which is the word of God;
praying always with all prayer and supplication in the Spirit…

EPHESIANS 6:10-18

A Time of Questions

Sometimes I enjoy talking to myself. Well, they do say it's good to talk to *somebody* intelligent at least once a day. But I've learned to be careful about what I say, especially if I'm giving myself the third degree, like a lawyer does in a courtroom. Or maybe I should say the thirty-question degree. I start asking myself questions and can't seem to stop. Have you ever...

- felt the world was closing in on you?
- wondered why your life is in chaos because you haven't done anything to cause it?
- questioned God about your pitiful circumstances?
- tried to figure out why people hurt you?
- whined about your physical condition?
- been financially broke?
- worried about your health?

- cried over a wayward child?
- blamed yourself for a failed relationship?
- found it hard to forgive someone who has wronged you?
- committed a sin that compromised your faith...but you deliberately keep doing it over and over?
- degraded or judged someone because of his or her sex, age, physical condition, or ethnicity?
- neglected to help someone you knew was in need?
- gossiped?
- caused embarrassment or shame?
- thought you had to perform for God to earn His love?
- manipulated other people—or even God—to get what you want?
- neglected, abandoned, or abused anyone—even yourself?
- considered yourself better or "less than" someone else?
- wanted something that didn't belong to you?
- been greedy?
- been jealous?
- embellished the truth?
- given more attention to something than you give to the Lord?
- tried to control the decisions and actions of other adults?
- encouraged or enticed someone to do the wrong thing?
- cheated any person, any business, or the government out of what you owe?
- used a mind-altering substance or an activity to cover up pain?
- struggled with self-esteem issues?

- been caught up in a fight that wasn't yours, but you were determined to win?

The Battle We're In

These questions reveal the trials and temptations we're involved with daily—things that let us know we're in a spiritual battle. This war is about whether our bodies, souls, and minds will be given over to evil. It's a battle against our human desires because we want to control life—to cajole people, situations, and circumstances to our preferences. We want to play God. No, baby, we want to be God. The answers to those thirty questions reveal how our self-centeredness and selfishness are personified—and how mercy, justice, grace, and favor can be nullified. Unfortunately we often leave little place for the Father, Son, and Holy Spirit to be manifest or magnified in our lives.

Our yes answers to those questions throw us into the hands of a game of mastery between God's way and the devil's ways. The end was determined before the foundation of the world, but our human nature is power hungry and wants to take over. And the devil gleefully hangs around to help. We work ourselves into a frenzy doing the very things that assure failure and disaster. We pick the wrong battles to fight and choose the wrong weapons of defense. We act like we're telling life, "Put up your dukes and fight!" We dare life to let us live *in* it, while what we really need to do is learn how to live successfully *through* it and glorify God.

I understand that fighting our desire for control isn't our natural inclination. One of the first laws of nature is self-preservation and taking the easiest route. And we often fool ourselves when we're busy handling our situations, thinking we know all the details and involvements and how to win in our own strength

On the other hand there are people who don't try to fight life's battles at all. They live in a state of apathy, denial, stubbornness, boredom, or defeat. There's no fight in them. They're unwilling to stand up to or for anything. They're waving the white flag and allowing themselves to be consumed in nothingness. They've even become numb to their feelings. They've lost the fight. Their bodies have deteriorated, their minds have petrified, their souls have experienced rigor mortis. Can these people choose to live again? What does God want for them?

Does Jesus Care?

Does Jesus care about the conditions and concerns we struggle with? Will the Holy Spirit work to bring life to dead or dying situations? *Yes!* None of the situations mentioned in the thirty questions are the real reasons for our struggles. Although our struggles are *in* life and *for* life, these are *symptoms* of a greater battle for our souls. All the conditions of hurt and hate have little to do with what's happening to us in our natural and physical existence. They're really about what's happening in our spirits.

Painful and heartbreaking situations in life should not surprise any of us. There's been pain for as long as there have been people, dating back to the Garden of Eden, when the first human beings broke their agreement with God. They disobeyed Him, and the struggle started then—and will continue until the final consummation of the ages.

Jesus reminds us that there's a life or death battle going on in the pastures of life where "the thief comes only to steal and kill and destroy" the sheep. But Jesus also promises, "I have come that [you] may have life, and have it to the full" (John 10:10 NIV).

So what are we going to do? We'll discover how to fight to win the spiritual war that rages in body, mind, and soul so we will be edified and God will be glorified.

Don't give in—God wants you to win!

1

Know How to Fight... but Never Start One

Through the elementary school grapevine, I got the word one day that Heddie Ruth was going to beat me up after school. I couldn't understand it. Heddie Ruth and I had grown up going to the same church and the same school. I thought we were good friends. So why didn't she like me now? Why was she mad at me? Why did she want to beat me up?

We both always tried to be the smartest students in class and make the highest grades. Did I score a higher grade in some subject than she did? Maybe she got upset thinking I was the teacher's pet (which I was). Maybe she thought I talked about her (which I didn't). Maybe some kid in class told her a lie about me.

Waiting for Me

I had no idea of the reason, but to hear the rumor mill talking about her wanting to fight me was disturbing. My great-grandmother, whom I lived with, had instilled in me that I should always be ladylike and that nice young ladies didn't lower themselves to fight. After school a crowd gathered to see what would happen between Heddie Ruth and me. I was as scared as I could be when I stepped through the only door we were permitted to go through to leave school. There she was, looking mad and talking trash like a heavyweight boxer.

I prayed, *Lord, please don't let her hit me. I don't know how to fight. I've never fought anybody in my life. I'll get a whipping if I fight because Granny told me I'd better not get into any trouble at school. And I've never been in trouble at school since I stole that dime in kindergarten. Help me, Lord!*

I had no choice but to make my way through the taunting crowd, get past my "friend," and then run home. *Here I go!* As I moved down the steps, Heddie Ruth hurled words I didn't understand. Then she balled up her fists and came after me. She got in a few good licks. I didn't fight back at all. Somehow I got away and ran all the way home.

When Granny saw me, she knew something was wrong. I explained to her what happened and, of course, she was shocked. It was her friend's granddaughter who was fighting me.

She assumed that whatever Heddie Ruth was angry about would be over by the next day. After all, Heddie Ruth was a nice girl and a friend of the family. Granny assured me I didn't have to be afraid when I went back to school the next day, and she told me to be friendly toward Heddie Ruth. But I didn't think it was over, and I didn't sleep too well that night.

All the next day I heard the same rumblings about Heddie Ruth wanting a fight, and this time the threats were stronger. What was I to do? *If I fight her I'll get in trouble, and if I don't fight her, the kids will laugh at me and call me names.* I certainly couldn't tell the teachers about it and have my classmates tease me for being a tattletale and coward. I was in a pickle. All day I worried but I never came up with a good plan.

Sure enough, after school the crowd assembled again outside the school door for the fight. My defense was no better than before, except this time I left my books at school so I could run faster. And I'd worn my tennis shoes that day so I could get better traction while running for my life.

Slowly I stepped down the stairs. With the loud roar of the crowd, Heddie Ruth came at me again to punch and scratch and speak trash. Once more I broke away and ran like I was running the fifty-yard dash.

The Truth Comes Out

At home Granny was waiting for me. I didn't have to tell her how things had gone; she could see the evidence. And now she was mad!

That's when the truth came out. "Thelma," she said with power and determination, "she's gonna be waiting on you tomorrow. I know I told you not to fight, but I meant for you not to *start* a fight. If she fights you tomorrow and you come home all beat up like you are today, I'm gonna whip you myself. You beat the fire out of her tomorrow. I don't care how you do it, but don't you let nobody make a fool out of you. You ain't no coward or no sissy. You're a young lady who's forced to defend yourself. So you think about how you're going to fight her tomorrow, and you come back here the winner."

Granny also stated her opinion that if I beat up Heddie Ruth just one time, she wouldn't bother me anymore. "She's just a bully, and the only way to stop bullies is to fight back and let them know you're not afraid of them. So get her tomorrow—or I'll get you."

Let me tell you, I'd rather fight Heddie Ruth any day than endure Granny's punishments. When Granny spanked me, she wasn't abusive—just firm and convincing. I knew she loved me when she spanked me because she tried to keep me from seeing her cry.

I stayed awake much of that night thinking how I was going to beat up Heddie Ruth the next day. When I got ready for school in the morning, I made sure my pigtails were criss-crossed and tied down with hairpins so she couldn't easily catch my hair.

Sure enough, the same situation was waiting for me after school. You'd think a teacher would have learned about this fighting business, but such fights were rare occurrences. And we lived in a safe and watching community, so the teachers didn't worry about us and stayed inside the school building.

When I walked out of the building and down the stairs where my rival was, I immediately caught her by surprise by punching her. I yanked her by the hair, and before she knew it she was on the ground and I was beating her up. I mean, I was winning this fight. Then she got loose and ran away, with all the kids laughing at her.

I didn't run home that day—I walked.

Granny was proud that I was the victor. The case was settled. Heddie Ruth and I became friends again, and all was well. And from that day until this, no one else has tried to fight me physically.

Looking back, I know that if I'd never gotten the courage to fight back, I would have lived in fear all the time. My ability to concentrate and do schoolwork would have been impaired. I would have been the laughingstock of the school, and this harmful reputation would have followed me the rest of my life. Doubt and fear would have been my daily companions. I would have been defeated for a long, long time—physically, emotionally, and spiritually.

How I Won

But I did fight back, and in doing so I won in three ways:

1. I never had to fight Heddie Ruth again.

2. My self-respect was restored.

3. I believe God gave me the strength to fight a good fight.

Granny taught me that God was in favor of us defending ourselves against enemies. I didn't consider Heddie Ruth my enemy, and I would never have thought of her that way had not her behavior toward me changed. But her harassment toward me was an illustration of life itself.

Jesus tells us in John 16:33 that we're going to have problems in this life. We'll be perplexed about some things. There'll be issues we don't understand. So-called friends will betray us, loved ones will disappoint us, others will lay traps for us, a few will lie about us, gossipers will scandalize our names, perpetrators will prey on us, relationships will be breached, and business deals will sour. We'll see leaders tarnished by greed, homes torn up by neglect, and children drawn away from their godly family heritage. Educational excellence will suffer, ungodly influences in pop culture will dictate our preferences, sickness and disease will be on the rise, crime will worsen, brutality and abuse will be commonplace, abductions and abandonments will increase, and financial difficulties will shock the proud. In many ways life will be described by this bumper sticker I saw: "Life is tough, and then you die!"

But there's another side to these situations! When Jesus says, "In the world you will have tribulation," He also says, *"But be of good cheer,* I have overcome the world" (John 16:33).

As long as we live we'll have adversity of one kind or another. "But"—and there's always something on the back of *but*—"be of good cheer!" When I first read that scripture, I didn't like how it sounded. Even in tribulation "be of good cheer" made no sense. *How can I be in a good mood when I'm broke or sick? Am I supposed to jump up and down with joy when my life's a mess? When I feel like I've been misused or I'm disappointed should I be happy?* I had absolutely no understanding of what God was saying.

My ignorance was not bliss. I was so unaware of the meaning of this passage that I missed the whole point made in the very next phrase: *I have overcome the world.* "I" who? Jesus—as God! The One in whom and through whom all things were created. He is the mighty God of this universe, the God who made heaven and earth, the God who formed man and woman from the dust of the earth and breathed His breath into us and we became living souls. He's the God who knows everything because He's the Alpha and the Omega, the Beginning and the End. He has promised us solace, a refuge in times of trouble, a shelter in times of storms. He is a safe harbor where no harm can overtake us. He's our avenger and defender. He's the One who speaks peace. When He speaks in our hearts, the peace of God, which we cannot explain, guards our hearts and our minds through Him (Philippians 4:6-7). And Jesus is our defense.

Granny gave me a plan of action against Heddie Ruth. She challenged me to fight or get spanked. She demanded that I defend myself or else. I'm so glad God doesn't issue that same edict. He doesn't place the burden of defending ourselves back on us. He doesn't tell us to set up our natural battle strategy and practice how we're going to punch and stomp and scratch and pull hair. He tells us to "chill"—to wait for Him to handle everything. In John 16:33 He assures us, "I have overcome the world."

To *overcome* means to struggle successfully against a difficulty or disadvantage, to make somebody hurting you incapacitated or helpless, to break down somebody's normal self-control, to defeat somebody or something, especially in a conflict or competition; to win or be successful, especially in spite of obstacles. In other words, God promises to *defeat* everything and everyone brought against you and me by the enemies of our lives and the enemy of our souls.

Now that calls for an *"Amen!"*

Fight Strategies

When I was planning to fight Heddie Ruth, I had no idea how to fight. I just used my imagination—stimulated by wrestling matches and prize fights I'd seen on television. I also drew on what I'd seen demonstrated in civil rights protests, cowboy movies, *Zorro,* and a few skirmishes at school. With all this in my mind to influence how

I thought I should fight, under the disguise of bravery I stepped out the school door and marched my way to victory.

Since then I've wondered about what goes into a good and fair fight. If I had to physically fight someone today (and I hope I never do), how could I be sure to come out the victor? Knowing *who* I was fighting, *why* I was fighting them, *where* and *when* to fight, and *what strategies* I could use would certainly be a good start.

These days plenty of schoolchildren are probably asking the same questions. According to a nationwide survey by the National Youth Violence Resource Center, one out of three students has been in a physical fight, and one out of eight has fought on school property. One of every twenty-five students has been hurt badly enough in a fight to need medical treatment. Many students today are designing their own strategies for the physical conflicts they face. Some are even carrying guns or other weapons to school. Yes, it's scary. But is there a bigger picture? The first law of nature is self-preservation. I wonder how many students are asking, *What should I preserve?* How many will actually strive to hang on to their privilege of pursuing a life of achievement and success? And how will they know how to fight the ills of our society and the attacks on their minds that come through mass media, family issues, peer pressure, financial struggles, educational challenges, and so forth?

Physically, mentally, and spiritually, adults are also fighting against weapons of mass destruction. And we continue to lose as many battles as the youth are. Against our adversities we often struggle as people who have no hope. We take matters into our own hands and mess things up—for ourselves as well as for everyone involved. We wish we could win, but we're not sure we can. We're toying with giving up. Thoughts of anger, dismay, despair, disgust, discord, devastation, deep-rooted sin, disappointment, deception, defiance, difficulties, disaster, disbelief, distractions, and devilment plague our minds. Why? Because we don't know how to fight.

If someone could take a sonogram of our hearts, they would find so many hurts. They would discover the emotional pain that makes us feel like we're choking, having a heart attack, or about to explode. These pains of the heart come from abuse, depression, sickness, disease, obsessive behavior, divorce, separation from loved ones, lack of forgiveness, lost dreams and goals, drug and alcohol abuse, moral decay, guilt, shame, embarrassment, lack of authenticity, hatred, jealousy, envy, strife, debauchery, and treachery. When we try to attack these heartaches by working them out ourselves or with advice of other hurting people, we lose almost every time.

We don't know how to fight effectively and well.

Often we try to rationalize our self-dependent approach to fighting. *God gave us a brain to think, so we should be able to work things out in a logical fashion.* Yeah, that really works, doesn't it? Not! Our logic is not God's logic, and God's logic isn't our logic. And what is logic anyway? Dictionaries define it in such phrases as "sensible, rational thought and argument rather than ideas that are influenced by emotion or whim" or "the relationship between specific events, situations, or objects, and the inevitable consequences of their interaction." Do we really have that kind of logic?

Questions...

- Are we smart enough to always see the next moment in our lives?

- Are we wise enough to realize the final consequences of our situation?

- Are we intelligent enough to always know the reactions of others?

- Are we so knowledgeable that we can combat any retaliation toward us?

- Are we clever enough to fully anticipate what our own reactions will be in certain situations?

- Are we arrogant enough to believe that people will change because we want them to?

- Are we intimidating enough to think people won't fight us back?

Baby, please! We don't know how to fight!

Strategies from the Experts

Sometimes we simply use the wrong weapons and strategies when we fight. Maybe we should apply these strategies I came across for street-smart self-defense: watch your back, stay on the alert, keep your hands in front of you, watch your mouth, keep a safe distance, injure vital parts of the attacker's body if you're attacked, yell for help, and escape as fast as you can. Or perhaps we should keep in mind the strategies promoted in a *Black Belt* magazine article by martial arts specialist Stefan Verstappen. He writes,

> Military history shows that battles are often won not by the biggest or fastest army, but by the commander who has the best strategy. The sparring arena is no different from the battleground. A slower and weaker fighter can beat a faster and stronger fighter if he is adept at using strategy.[1]

This article highlights three ancient Chinese strategies handed down from ages past:

> *Create Something from Nothing:* Use the same feint twice. Having reacted to the first and often the second as well, the enemy will be hesitant to react to a third feint. Therefore, the third feint is the actual attack catching your enemy with his guard down...

Lure the Tiger Down the Mountain: Never directly attack a well entrenched opponent. Instead lure him away from his stronghold and separate him from his source of strength...

Await the Exhausted Enemy at Your Ease: Encourage your enemy to expend his energy in futile quests while you conserve your strength. When he is exhausted and confused, you attack with energy and purpose...

That last one is especially important when we're facing "an opponent who is confident and aggressive and who also has a lot of energy." It requires a patient response of retreat and defense while the opponent attacks. And then...

after a few minutes you will notice the attacker's techniques becoming sloppy, which indicates he's already tired. This is the time to reverse the roles and move in with as much speed and power as you have. The attacker, tired and used to only seeing you retreat and defend, will be caught by surprise and [be] defeated by a sudden counter-attack.

This article concludes by saying that martial artists "must learn to become a living weapon—one who battles opponents not only in the physical arena, but on psychological and spiritual levels as well." Now that's surely worth thinking about.

Another approach we might try is the advice in an *Esquire* magazine article entitled "The Fistfight: A Primer."[2] The article first says *not* to fight because we're too smart for that. We should look for a way out. But if we must fight, we should remember such things as taking off our glasses and coats, not breaking our fingers when we punch, getting close to our opponent's head if we're going to butt it, using our elbows, utilizing gravity if we're large, and remembering that we're not in the movies.

With detailed advice like this, are you ready to take on opponents?

I don't think so.

We can use fighting strategies from many books and think we're so informed, but we'll probably end up losing our shirts, our teeth, or our lives.

Deciding Not to Fight

On a couple of occasions some of my family members have been upset with me because I didn't fight back. A few years ago a doctor admitted that he'd made some serious mistakes during a surgery I'd undergone. His mistakes caused me severe agony, and I'm still feeling some negative effects. I thought long and hard about suing this doctor and the hospital. I realized I had a legal right to sue them. I'd already received the doctor's verbal confirmation that he made errors. He even said if I wanted to sue him, he understood. (He was repentant and remorseful.)

After prayerful consideration, I announced to my family that I was not going to pursue this any further. Things got really silent in the room. I could cut the disdain with a knife. One family member said coldly, "I knew you were going to do that." Another argued with me several times. Just a few months ago, I received a letter from another family member who was still perplexed by my action. The letter noted I'd never be rich because I didn't know how to fight for what's mine. I'd also spoken with several friends about the situation, and one of them, like my family, adamantly disagreed with my chosen response.

When faced with big decisions and when I want a word from the Lord, I go to Debra, my spiritual accountability partner, knowing she won't tell me or advise me on anything until she first goes before the Lord Jesus Christ. After much prayer and meditation, she shared with me, "God is pleased with you. He will repay!"

Another time I had a dispute with a business entity. I knew they weren't being fair, and I was ready to fight them legally with everything I had. I went away for a week to fast and pray, expecting to return home with the strategy for winning the case. I waited for God to pour everything out so I could fight, but for seven days I received no strategy from Him—or at least not the one I was expecting. God kept speaking to my mind in a sound bite: "Trust Me. Trust Me."

So I came back home with only one strategy to fight with: trust in God. I didn't sue. In fact, I didn't respond to the other party at all. I just trusted God. This went on for eight months. They didn't bother me, and I didn't bother them. I waited patiently on the Lord.

During the eighth month of patience, God spoke again and said, "Now!" I knew what it meant. I picked up the telephone and spoke to the correct person. I asked that a revised contract I submitted be signed that day and sent to me the following day. Without further conversation, I received my signed contract before the deadline.

During this time, my friend Debra kept writing to me. She reminded me that God doesn't change: "He's not fickle. He's not moody. He is not schizophrenic. He doesn't beat you over the head one minute and then pat you on it the next." She reminded me of Psalm 20:7: "Some trust in chariots, and some in horses; but we will remember the name of the LORD our God." Debra wrote, "Safety is of the Lord...Even with all the horses and chariots prepared for life, health, battle—deliverance and safety are only from the One True God. Hallelujah! How faithful He is. Praise His name forever. Glory to God for His faithfulness breaking out in our lives...step-by-step, day-by-day in every way."

Sustaining Scriptures

When you want to fight and don't know how, sustaining Scriptures are necessary, such as all of Psalm 20 NIV:

> May the LORD answer you when you are in distress;
> may the name of the God of Jacob protect you.
> May he send you help from the sanctuary
> and grant you support from Zion.

May he remember all your sacrifices
and accept your burnt offerings.
May he give you the desire of your heart
and make all your plans succeed.
We will shout for joy when you are victorious
and will lift up our banners in the name of our God.
May the LORD grant all your requests.
Now I know that the LORD saves his anointed;
he answers him from his holy heaven
with the saving power of his right hand.
Some trust in chariots and some in horses,
but we trust in the name of the LORD our God.
They are brought to their knees and fall,
but we rise up and stand firm.
O LORD, save the king!
Answer us when we call!

If you had to fight now, would you feel confident?

PROPERTY OF
BROADWAY CHRISTIAN CHURCH LIBRARY
910 BROADWAY
FORT WAYNE, IN 46802

2

Fight or Flight?

Everybody is born with the will to "be better." We all have this basic instinct because we all have the desire to win, or be successful. Behavioral scientists speak of our "basic human drives." Here's a list that one psychologist put together of sixteen "core drives"—the "core drives and desires that motivate humans to do the things we do":

1. sex/romance
2. acquisition/saving
3. bonding/connecting
4. learning/curiosity
5. eating
6. defense/fight-or-flight
7. nesting
8. vengeance

9. status

10. power

11. loyalty

12. order and organization

13. independence

14. acceptance

15. altruism

16. physical activity[1]

Did you see that defending ourselves—with flight or flight—is on that list—at number 6? How can we win if we don't defend ourselves and fight with all our might to secure what we want in life? I'm sure you've seen it in babies. Watching my 11 grandchildren (including 3 great-grands!) I've noticed they fight for attention, possession, and achievement.

Fight or Flight Observations

When my oldest grandchild was in elementary school he was mischievous. This really came out as he learned how to defend himself from boredom. Because he's very smart and could do his work in less time than the teachers assigned, he would finish his tasks quickly and accurately and then harass and interrupt the other children by pulling on their hair, talking to them, or something else that distracted them and eventually got the teacher's attention. Then my grandson would get suspended for several days or receive some other discipline such as detention. Bless his heart, he didn't know how to express the fact that he needed more to challenge his intellect, so he invoked two defense techniques. He fought by bothering the children or doing something to get attention, knowing he would be sent home for several days, which rewarded him with a flight defense. It meant he could be out of that classroom and away from boredom for a while.

Was he ready to win? He wanted to win, but he used the wrong techniques. Consequently he was shifted from school to school in several school districts, because nobody caught on that all he needed was more challenge and stimulation to keep him focused on his schoolwork.

As his grandmother I tried to help him, but I didn't really know what to do. So I went to the school often to see what he was up to. I talked to the teachers and suggested they give him more work to do and allow him to help some of the other students. I don't think that lasted long because he would tease the kids he was helping. (Yes, he was mischievous. I said that already.)

He knew full well what would get him suspended. Realizing that, I asked the principal to not do that anymore…but instead "sentence" him to a corner of the library with his back turned to the children and teachers. He could read books or work on projects. That way the teachers could keep their eyes on him but he wouldn't bother anyone. That worked for a short while, but because he's so sharp, he learned how to beat that too—He acted like he was repentant and reformed until they stopped the discipline, and then he went back to square one and caused trouble again.

My grandson is now a grown, married man with two daughters. He's very well adjusted and motivated. He has a job he doesn't mind getting up to go to, a wife who's as intelligent as he is (he likes that), and children who are also very smart. Because of his childhood experiences, he's able to direct his own children to different, more appropriate defense mechanisms than those he tried. I guess he did learn something from his past. He's even teaching his baby brother, who's four years old, to use better defenses than throwing temper tantrums, whining, and acting up when he doesn't get what he wants.

I've also watched my oldest granddaughter deal with some questionable times in her life. As a teenager she decided to fight her disappointments and struggles by choosing friends who weren't the best influences. Her grades suffered, and she started getting rebellious. Her parents were concerned with how she was acting. Fortunately her relationship with them was solid enough that they could talk with her about these things.

They also invited me to help by talking with her. She'd accepted Christ as her Savior, and He caused her heart to be open to hearing wise counsel. After one of our serious grandmother/granddaughter discussions, she told her mom, "Grammy sure knows how to make me feel bad." Well, Grammy wasn't trying to make her feel bad, but it sure helps when Grammy prays to God for guidance and obeys what He tells her to do. I spoke to my grandchild from the Word of God about what she needed and blended it together with a little of what my great-grandmother told me. These words of life and encouragement made a huge difference because she listened.

All she was trying to do was find a way to win over what she considered hard times. She didn't really know the practicalities of fight or flight. She knew she needed guidance, but she didn't know how to ask because she didn't think anyone would understand. Today her grades are great. She's a member of the National Honor Society and a captain on the Step Team. She attends church regularly and is involved in other wholesome activities.

Learning how to ask for and listen to wise counsel helps us know how to be ready to fight to win.

My next-to-oldest granddaughter is a talented athlete who's really into basketball. At her birth, the umbilical cord was wrapped twice around her neck and she nearly died. The doctors believed she would have some brain damage. Not so! This girl is as clever and intelligent as she can be. (All my children and grandchildren are brilliant. Okay, so I'm their grandmother and might be a little biased, but I'm truthful too.) She's also in the National Honor Society and is proficient in playing the piano and other activities.

As I've watched how she handles fight or flight situations I've realized she's a "crying woman." When she's not satisfied with something, she'll hang her head, drag her feet, and become silent. Big teardrops nestle in her eyes or trickle down her light bronze cheeks until someone asks, "What's the matter, baby?" To which she'll say, "Nothing," and return to her fight or flight performance again, just waiting until you ask her one more time—and then she'll comment, "Well, I'll tell you…" Then the conversation becomes informative. Her mind is also open to wise counsel.

My grandkids know they can always come to Grammy, because they know I'll steer them in the right direction—sometimes in a direction of correction, sometimes in a direction of a better understanding of their situation, sometimes in a direction of silence. I'm always praying that God will give me the right words to say and the right action to do because I want them to win.

My other seven little grandkids also have their individual personalities and fight or flight techniques. I love watching them express themselves. One is a beautiful dancer and into sports as well. She absorbs herself in her studies, basketball, and Christian interpretive dancing. She's happy and well-adjusted—until she gets hungry. Her total personality changes when she wants to eat. Hunger pushes her over the brink. That's when her "fight" comes to the forefront. She's grouchy, moody, cranky, tearful, and agitated until she gets something in her stomach. All those moods are part of her defenses, and until she's fed she won't study or participate in anything other than watching television. I see her in her different moods and then retreating to the television to escape the waiting period of food preparation. That's real fight or flight drama if I've ever seen it.

Another grandchild is a recluse. She's never been one to hang out with her sisters or cousins. She enjoys being by herself in her own world, and she seldom invites others in. She frequently asks

people out of her room, locks the door, and is perfectly content
doing what she wants to do when she wants to do it, without anyone else's participation. On the other hand, when she wants to be
with people she emerges, interacts appropriately, laughs, talks, and
integrates for a while—until she gets enough and retreats back to the
sanctuary of her space. I don't know whether this is fight or flight or
just living the life she enjoys. But I do know this: More than any of
the others, this grandbaby reminds me of my own natural mother,
though I wasn't well acquainted with her. My mother enjoyed company when she wanted it but would ask you to go home when she got
tired of you. People knew she was like that, and they knew she was
just being honest, not mean. Nor is my granddaughter necessarily
mean when she's most honest about what she wants and gets it.

The four youngest grandbabies—ranging in age from three
years old down to three months—have a ways to go before I can see
indications of their fight or flight methods. However, I can see some
of the techniques typical of most little ones. When they put up their
defenses they cry, pout, throw, snatch, hit, or fall on the floor. They
reach for their pacifiers, get distracted by something or somebody,
or run into somebody's safe arms.

Hmm...now I'm thinking about that last one: *Run into safe
arms*. Do you think we can learn how to win from the innocence of
little babies? Is Jesus giving us insight about running into safe arms
when He tells the disciples, "Truly, I say to you, unless you turn and
become like children, you will never enter the kingdom of heaven.
Whoever humbles himself like this child is the greatest in the kingdom of heaven" (Matthew 18:3-4 ESV). How profound! Jesus advises
us to become humble—to be trusting and forgiving in our bodies,
minds, and spirits—just as little children are if we're going to win.

I watch these little children tussling, biting, hitting, fussing,
and then a few seconds later they're playing with each other as if
none of that happened. How many adults can honestly say they
reconcile that quickly?

What fight or flight responses can you see in yourself and in those around you? What can you learn about coping skills and winning from your observations?

Humble Enough to Win

Winning is not about brilliance or intelligence. It's really about humbling ourselves before the mighty hand of God, trusting in Him with all our soul and mind, forgiving ourselves and others for everything done to us, and seeking forgiveness for everything we've done to others. It's about keeping our mind on Jesus, walking in righteousness, understanding the truth of God, praying with all sincerity, being prepared with the Word of God in our spirit, and being covered by our unwavering faith in God. The innocence of a child can be the strength of an adult who really wants to succeed.

This makes me want to sing!

> What a fellowship, what a joy divine,
> Leaning on the everlasting arms;
> What a blessedness, what a peace is mine,
> Leaning on the everlasting arms.
>
> Leaning, leaning, safe and secure from all alarms;
> Leaning, leaning, leaning on the everlasting arms.
>
> O how sweet to walk in this pilgrim way,
> Leaning on the everlasting arms;
> O how bright the path grows from day to day,
> Leaning on the everlasting arms.
>
> What have I to dread, what have I to fear,
> Leaning on the everlasting arms;
> I have blessed peace with my Lord so near,
> Leaning on the everlasting arms.[2]

Sometimes I just have to sing about winning! This is my natural, emotional, and spiritual desire: *To win!*

They Had Everything

The biblical record of humanity's beginning in this world is one of complete openness. There was no shame and guilt, no hidden agendas, no need to dominate or control. There were no secrets, no fear, no antagonism, no need for forgiveness, no aggression, no agitation, no depression, no oppression, no hostility, no anger, no bitterness, no vengeance, no reviling, no name-calling, no plotting and planning harm, no bullying, no cajoling, no deceit, no envy, no jealousy, no coveting, no manipulating, no competition, no debt, no violence, no pettiness, no politics, no hiding, no neglect, no pouting, no ugliness, no dishonesty, no immorality, no lying, no gossiping, no backbiting, no vices, no cheating. Think of it: There was no sin on this earth!

When God created Adam and completed him with Eve, Adam sealed his completeness by saying to God, "This is now bone of my bones, and flesh of my flesh; she shall be called Woman, because she was taken out of Man" (Genesis 2:23). The two of them were complete and wholesome, fulfilled in their relationship with each other as well as with God, all in a way that nothing else could supply. They were completely innocent, humble, and trusting.

The Bible is clear in teaching us that mankind was morally free at this time—and their free choices were morally significant. Adam and Eve were the epitome and personification of those sixteen basic needs we saw at the beginning of this chapter, except that all the elements of a winner were innate in them—for God breathed into man and they became living souls. *The breath of God was everything man and woman needed.*

The first biblical humans understood that their purpose was to take care of the creation—as beautifully shown when Adam assigned names to all the living creatures. Yes, Adam and Eve understood nature and purpose. They were to fellowship with their Creator as creatures in His image. And along with this responsibility and privilege came a command to be obeyed: They were *not* to eat of the "tree of the knowledge of good and evil" (Genesis 2:16-17). In this arrangement were Adam and Eve winning? Yes!

And so I'm convinced that each one of us already has in us the spirit of winning God's way. It's the same spirit that enters into a mother's womb and is knit together by the mighty hand of God with all the faculties, organs, systems, muscles, nerves, and extremities needed for us to be complete in the three parts of our beings— body, soul, and spirit.

I am persuaded by the words of God recorded in the Holy Bible that before the foundation of the world God called us *winners*. And everything He does is to help us live up to that name. What is true about all of us is expressed in these words David, a man after God's heart, spoke to his Creator:

> For You formed my inward parts;
> You covered me in my mother's womb.
> I will praise You, for I am fearfully and wonderfully made;
> Marvelous are Your works,
> And that my soul knows very well.
> My frame was not hidden from You,
> When I was made in secret,
> And skillfully wrought in the lowest parts of the earth.
> Your eyes saw my substance, being yet unformed.
> And in Your book they all were written,
> The days fashioned for me,
> When as yet there were none of them.
> How precious also are Your thoughts to me, O God!
> How great is the sum of them! (Psalm 139:13-17).

Wow! These truths David reveals mean that God knows all about us. There's nothing hidden from Him. As Jesus told us, as recorded in Matthew 10:30, God our Father knows how many hairs there are on our heads!

Fearfully and Wonderfully

When we read that God has made us "fearfully and wonderfully," what is really being said? When He made us, God made no mistakes. Hallelujah! God created us as His kingdom children, and He rules in us from our minds, which is the first part of our development as babies—our brains. God covered us, or fenced us in, with our individual emotions while we were still in our mothers' wombs. We can praise God and rejoice because we can morally revere Him and stand in awe of Him as our Creator. We were made to be wonderfully distinguished and marvelously separated from the things that pull us down. We can be exceedingly excellent in the ways of God because we're fearfully and wonderfully made. Glory to God! Are you getting this? You were made to win.

But something else happened in the Garden of Eden that changed the entire course of God's original nature for us. It shifted our course, spinning the work of God and the world into a different dispensation, a different time, a period of hardship and trials.

We all probably know the story of Lucifer. If you don't, you know of his works in the world. He wreaks havoc. Just look around and you'll see his devastation in the weather, in mean and cantankerous people, in business fraud, in breakdowns in religion, in obscenities in the media, in the acceptance of immorality, in unprecedented numbers of divorces, in tumbling self-esteem, in crumbling politics, in breakdowns of systems, and in problems everywhere that seem to have no solution. All these were originally set in motion by the disobedience of the two most perfect people who lived in a perfect world.

The Tragic Story

Read about it for yourself. I'm including the whole tragic story here because it's so instructive for us and worth revisiting often.

Now the serpent was more cunning than any beast of the field which the Lord God had made. And he said to the woman, "Has God indeed said, 'You shall not eat of every tree of the garden'?"

And the woman said to the serpent, "We may eat the fruit of the trees of the garden; but of the fruit of the tree which is in the midst of the garden, God has said, 'You shall not eat it, nor shall you touch it, lest you die.' "

Then the serpent said to the woman, "You will not surely die. For God knows that in the day you eat of it your eyes will be opened, and you will be like God, knowing good and evil."

So when the woman saw that the tree was good for food, that it was pleasant to the eyes, and a tree desirable to make one wise, she took of its fruit and ate. She also gave to her husband with her, and he ate. Then the eyes of both of them were opened, and they knew that they were naked; and they sewed fig leaves together and made themselves coverings.

And they heard the sound of the Lord God walking in the garden in the cool of the day, and Adam and his wife hid themselves from the presence of the Lord God among the trees of the garden.

Then the Lord God called to Adam and said to him, "Where are you?"

So he said, "I heard Your voice in the garden, and I was afraid because I was naked; and I hid myself."

And He said, "Who told you that you were naked? Have you eaten from the tree of which I commanded you that you should not eat?"

Then the man said, "The woman whom You gave to be with me, she gave me of the tree, and I ate."

And the Lord God said to the woman, "What is this you have done?" The woman said, "The serpent deceived me, and I ate."

So the Lord God said to the serpent:

> "Because you have done this,
> You are cursed more than all cattle,
> And more than every beast of the field;
> On your belly you shall go,
> And you shall eat dust all the days of your life.
> And I will put enmity
> Between you and the woman,
> And between your seed and her Seed;
> He shall bruise your head,
> And you shall bruise His heel."

To the woman He said: "I will greatly multiply your sorrow and your conception; in pain you shall bring forth children; your desire shall be for your husband, and he shall rule over you."

Then to Adam He said, "Because you have heeded the voice of your wife, and have eaten from the tree of which I commanded you, saying, 'You shall not eat of it':

> "Cursed is the ground for your sake;
> In toil you shall eat of it
> All the days of your life.
> Both thorns and thistles it shall bring forth for you,
> And you shall eat the herb of the field.
> In the sweat of your face you shall eat bread
> Till you return to the ground,
> For out of it you were taken;
> For dust you are,
> And to dust you shall return."

And Adam called his wife's name Eve, because she was the mother of all living.

Also for Adam and his wife the Lord God made tunics of skin, and clothed them.

Then the Lord God said, "Behold, the man has become like one of Us, to know good and evil. And now, lest he put out his hand and take also of the tree of life, and eat, and live forever"—

therefore the LORD God sent him out of the garden of Eden to till the ground from which he was taken. So He drove out the man; and He placed cherubim at the east of the garden of Eden, and a flaming sword which turned every way, to guard the way to the tree of life (Genesis 3).

From this situation, what Jesus said in John 10:10 becomes clear: "The thief does not come except to steal, and to kill, and to destroy." Do you understand what this thief (our enemy—the devil) is doing? He comes to make sure we lose the battles we're up against in this life on earth. He wants to steal our joy, to kill God's plans and dreams for us, and to destroy our lives completely. Just as Eve did, we can fall to the lies and traps of Satan and become victimized by his schemes, which Scripture calls "the wiles of the devil" (Ephesians 6:11).

By falling for the schemes and plots that have been formed against us, many people fight against what God has planned for them. They use fight or flight methods that can destroy them, their families, their careers, their goals and dreams, and their successes— every good thing God prepared for them.

When people resort to being abusive, using alcohol and drugs, embezzling, becoming sexually intimate with different people, stealing, and other similar activities, they're fighting against and trying to flee from the tribulations they're experiencing in their lives.

This kind of fighting is always, without question, detrimental to all involved. It's impossible to win with these kinds of behaviors, and we fall deeper into the schemes of the devil when we succumb.

Schemes of Satan

Take a look at these truths about the devil's agenda compiled by Reb Bradley of Family Ministries.[3]

1. What is Satan's overall goal? *To advance his kingdom—to extend his sphere of influence.* (See John 14:30; 16:11; Ephesians 2:2; 2 Corinthians 4:4; 1 John 3:12; 5:19; Acts 26:18.)

2. What is Satan's primary scheme? *To distract us from our pure and sincere devotion to Christ—and remove us from the battle.* (See 2 Corinthians 11:3.)

3. By what means does Satan wage his warfare? Look closely at the different schemes of his that go along with his various goals:

Satan's Goal Is to Destroy Our Faith

And these are his schemes for doing it:

- Tempt us into sin (Genesis 3:1-6; Matthew 4:3; Luke 4:2; John 13:2; Acts 5:3) by defiling our conscience (1 Timothy 1:19) and getting a foothold (Ephesians 4:26-27).

- Persecute believers (1 Peter 5:8-9; Revelation 2:10,13).

- Trip us up by slander (Genesis 3:1; Matthew 4:1-3; Luke 22:3-4).

- Draw us into self-reliance (1 Timothy 3:6-7; 2 Timothy 2:26; 1 Corinthians 10:12; 1 Corinthians 3:18-19).

- Get our eyes off Christ (Hebrews 12:1-3; Luke 9:62).

- Catch us off guard (Luke 4:1-2; 1 Peter 5:8).

Satan's Goal Is to Demoralize Us

And these are his methods:

- Accuse the saints (Revelation 12:10-11; Zechariah 3:1; 1 John 2:1; Romans 8:33; Job 1) by condemning us (Romans 8:1; 5:10) and intimidating us (Luke 4:3; Romans 8:15).

- Discourage us (Luke 4:9-11; 2 Corinthians 2:6-11).

Satan's Goal Is to Redefine the Battle

The devil wants to—

- Make us think there is no battle, that the devil is nonexistent or irrelevant (Acts 23:8).

- Promote exclusivism, tempting other believers to become our opponents (1 Corinthians 3:4-5).

- Make the battle a "fleshly" one—encouraging us to use our own efforts to achieve spiritual ends (Luke 4:6-7; 1 Chronicles 21:1; Matthew 26:51-52).

- Have us battle for power and authority (Genesis 3:5; Jude 4,8-10).

Satan's Goal Is to Bring Division

The devil fosters—

- Unresolved anger, unforgiveness, bitterness (Ephesians 4:26-31; Ephesians 4:3).

- Envy, pride, selfish ambition (James 3:14-15).

- Covetousness, murder, arguments (James 4:1-2).

- Bad judgment, slander, gossip, inflammatory speech (James 4:11; Ephesians 4:31; Colossians 3:8).

- Alienation from leaders by sowing seeds of mistrust (Genesis 3:4-5; 1 Samuel 15:23; Numbers 16:11).

Satan's Goal Is to Deceive Us

And these are his schemes for doing it:

- Lies (John 8:44; 2 Corinthians 11:3; Revelation 16:14; 20:7-8).

- Twisting the truth (2 Corinthians 11:14; Genesis 3:5; Matthew 4:6).

- Targeting God's people (Matthew 24:24).

Satan's Goal Is to Lead Us into Error

Satan provides:

- False teachers (1 Timothy 4:1-2; Galatians 3:1; 4:17; 2 Timothy 4:3-4).

- False teaching (2 Corinthians 10:4-5; 11:3-4).

- False miracles (2 Thessalonians 2:9-12; Revelation 16:14; 19:20; Matthew 7:22-23).

- Ammunition for shooting down (targeting) good leaders (Acts 20:28-31; 3 John 9-10).

Satan's Goal Is to Gain Direct Influence over Us

He does this through—

- Blatant occultism (Luke 4:5-7).

- Veiled occultism—"New Age" and Christian mysticism (Acts 19:19; Acts 15:19-20; Acts 8:18-20; Genesis 3:5).

- Attempting to demonize believers (Matthew 12:43; Ephesians 4:26-27; Matthew 16:22-23).

Satan's Goal Is to Prevent Conversion to Christianity

The devil wants to—

- Steal seeds of the gospel (Matthew 13:4,19).

- Blind unbelievers (2 Corinthians 4:4).

Satan's Goal Is to Dilute Christian Efforts

He wants to get us to—

- Mix the phony with the real (Matthew 13:24-25,38-39; Acts 20:29-30; Jude 4; 1 John 4:3).

- Change the church's agenda (Luke 22:3; John 12:5-6; Matthew 27:3-5).[3]

Satan Will Not Be Successful Long Term

Yes, the devil's schemes and strategies are complex and comprehensive. But know this: If a person who indulges in any of these vices or falls prey to any of these devilish strategies is determined to change his or her behavior, then he or she will win by turning to Christ for help and following His lead. Why? Because the Word of God says to those who believe in God that no weapon formed against them will prosper or be successful (Isaiah 54:17). This is great news from the Word of God!

This gives me hope...I hope it does the same for you!

3

Breakdown for a Blessing

At one time I came close to having a nervous breakdown. During that dilemma I had fainting spells and would fall down. When I finally went to the doctor to see what was wrong, he asked me a series of questions:

- "What happens when you faint?"

- "Do you know what's going on around you while you're out?"

- "Can you hear people talking while you're out?"

My answer to those last two questions was yes. Then the doctor said, "You didn't faint. People who really faint don't know what's going on around them."

Evidently that called for another examination of the psychological kind. After several days in the hospital seeing one specialist after another, they determined I was having some kind of mental episodes. I wasn't quite crazy, but if I didn't take action, I would eventually get worse. As I followed the doctors' advice and made some life changes, I was grateful for experts who could diagnose disorders and treat them properly. I needed no medication, just some rethinking and redirecting of my life.

Nearly over the Brink

That was the first episode. Now I faced a new one. For days I was irritable, having chest pains, choking a lot, and food was hard to swallow. I was crying about anything and everything. I didn't feel like talking to people or going home or taking care of my family. I resented all the requirements of marriage. I finally realized this was partly a continuation of feelings of inadequacy augmented by fresh, negative revelations concerning a person I dearly love. I was about to be pushed over the brink.

At the time I had a great job as assistant vice president of a prestigious bank. I also was teaching banking for the American Institute of Banking in several locations around the country. I was a successful community worker and church officer. I had enough material possessions for my family and me to be comfortable because, along with the money I was making, my husband was a great provider.

I knew how to look like everything was okeydoke. I was fooling people with an "I'm so happy" pretense. No one suspected my heart was torn in little shreds and bleeding profusely from disappointment, guilt, shame, embarrassment, and fear.

Things were a mess on the homefront. I'd gotten confirmation on some hurtful things that had happened during my marriage, and I finally came to accept that I had a child in trouble. But there was nobody for me to talk to about these issues because my best confidants—my great-grandmother and my granddaddy—were now dead. I had nowhere to run, nobody to hold me, nobody to tell me, "It's going to be all right." Remember that bumper sticker I mentioned earlier? "Life is tough and then you die!" Was I dying now?

It's true. Life is tough. Babies don't know how good they have it. They cry and they get attention. When they're upset, they get noticed. When they fall down, they get picked up. They have all these needs, and those needs get met. What a life...for a while. Then they grow up and realize that things are really not as great as they appear. Life *is* hard. Life is often disappointing and sometimes suffocating.

I knew quite well how to play the "I'm fine" game. After crying most of the night for many nights, my day would go something like this: Six a.m.: get up and clean up, put on clothes (I was a very sharp dresser with fashionable corporate attire. I looked like I stepped out of a business fashion magazine), put on makeup, eat a little breakfast, think about what needed to be done that day, fill a baggy with ice chips and wrap a towel around it, get the car keys, go outside, get into the car, and drive to work at the bank. I didn't want the hurts I was experiencing to follow me, but as soon as I'd get into the car I'd start crying. My tears would overflow, making my eyes red and my face swollen, destroying my makeup and dignity. That's what the ice was for. I'd drive to work holding that little bag of ice on my eyes, alternating from one eye to the other until I got to work. This kept my eyes and face from looking like I'd been on a drinking binge all night.

I was determined to keep secret all that was going on in my life. For doing that, I had another survival tool along with the ice baggy—makeup. My makeup kit had everything I needed—concealer, rouge (that's what we called it then; now they call it blush), powder, eyeliner, and lipstick. I would park my car under the covered parking lot in the shopping center next to where I worked. With my lighted mirror on, I'd correct the damage brought on by the tears and sorrow. Then it was "happy face" time. The smile was plastered on my face, my brain was kicked into don't-compete-with-the-work-at-the-bank gear.

I talked to myself (as any self-respecting woman with a problem does). I directly addressed my problems:

> Today is another day of work, and I will not take you into the building with me. You will stay in this car. If it's hot, I hope you smother; if it's cold, I hope you freeze to death. But you will *not* follow me inside. I'll be back this evening, and if you're still here, I'll see you then. Goodbye!

Off I'd go to start another day of work—and lies. When people asked me how I was, I'd say, "Wonderful! It couldn't be better." (Liar, liar, pants on fire.) I was dying on the inside and lying on the outside.

This went on for weeks and weeks. I was angry and had become bitter about my marriage. I was scared and upset because of my child's behavior. I was lonesome for my Granny and Daddy Lawrence. I was afraid to talk about what was happening with anyone at the church or in the community. I knew there were people who loved me, but because of their closeness to the situations I didn't want to reveal truths that would upset them. I also was embarrassed and perplexed.

What Was I to Do?

In the midnight hours, when my heart was breaking, I read my Bible and called out to God. Praying was so natural for me. I grew up talking to and praising God. My life had always been centered and covered with communication with Him. But now it didn't seem to make a lot of difference. Things stayed the same, and my disappointment and sorrow became deeper the more I thought about them.

I remembered some advice from when I had the fainting problems. My doctor told me to watch what I say and emphasized how important words are in dealing with self-esteem. He told me to think positively about myself. Every time I thought or said something negative about myself, I was to immediately eradicate it with a positive. He even gave me a list of what to say:

- I like myself.

- Things work out for me.

- I am well and healthy.

- I have all the money I need to do everything I want.

- I am beautiful.

- I am happy.

- I am loved.

Using this list helped me earlier to build my confidence. So I tried it again in this situation, but with only minimal effect. I'm positive that reading my Bible and praying helped me keep my sanity, in spite of the choking and hyperventilating. But it was far from the healing and deliverance I needed to experience in order to survive…and win.

> *O God, what am I to do?* This was my constant plea. *What am I supposed to do?*
> *How can I make it through this?*
> *Life is not supposed to be like this!*
> *I thought when I became a Christian at age four nothing but good things would come my way. Isn't that the reward for knowing and following You?*

How misled we can be by some of the teachings we sit under. That's why it's so important to study the Bible.

Staring at Tribulation

If we were *not* going to face hurts and disappointments and all the stuff we go through in life, do you think God would have had John write down these words of Jesus:

> These things I have spoken to you, that in Me you may have peace. *In the world you will have tribulation;* but be of good cheer, I have overcome the world (John 16:33).

These words are included in the Bible because the Lord knew we were going to go through some awful stuff on our way to eternal life spent in His presence.

If anybody had told me earlier that tribulation would feel like I felt in this time of testing and cause me to act like I was acting, I wouldn't have been able to identify with it. But now here was tribulation as real as could be and in living color. Not as a preview of coming attractions, but as the real show. And I didn't like it at all. That's why my heart's cry was, *Lord, what am I to do?*

A Breakthrough

After praying and crying and studying, and crying and praying, and crying some more, I finally got a breakthrough one morning while holding a bag of ice to one eye and driving to work. I know it was the Holy Spirit that morning who clearly told me to read Psalm 27, and to read it on the phone with my troubled child. I was eager to make that call, but I had to wait till I got to work. My tears stopped flowing and the choking subsided. When I reached the parking lot, I had little need for redoing my makeup. I got out of the car that morning with more pep in my step than I'd had for months. I was really smiling!

As soon as I stepped into the bank and my hands could touch the phone and grab a Bible, I called my child. We read Psalm 27 in the King James Version:

> The LORD is my light and my salvation; whom shall I fear? The LORD is the strength of my life; of whom shall I be afraid?
>
> When the wicked, even mine enemies and my foes, came upon me to eat up my flesh, they stumbled and fell.

Though an host should encamp against me, my heart shall not fear: though war should rise against me, in this will I be confident.

One thing have I desired of the LORD, that will I seek after; that I may dwell in the house of the LORD all the days of my life, to behold the beauty of the LORD, and to inquire in his temple.

For in the time of trouble he shall hide me in his pavilion: in the secret of his tabernacle shall he hide me; he shall set me up upon a rock.

And now shall mine head be lifted up above mine enemies round about me: therefore will I offer in his tabernacle sacrifices of joy; I will sing, yea, I will sing praises unto the LORD.

Hear, O LORD, when I cry with my voice: have mercy also upon me, and answer me.

When thou saidst, Seek ye my face; my heart said unto thee, Thy face, LORD, will I seek.

Hide not thy face far from me; put not thy servant away in anger: thou hast been my help; leave me not, neither forsake me, O God of my salvation.

When my father and my mother forsake me, then the LORD will take me up.

Teach me thy way, O LORD, and lead me in a plain path, because of mine enemies.

Deliver me not over unto the will of mine enemies: for false witnesses are risen up against me, and such as breathe out cruelty.

I had fainted, unless I had believed to see the goodness of the LORD in the land of the living.

Wait on the LORD: be of good courage, and he shall strengthen thine heart: wait, I say, on the LORD.

Wow! That was the beginning of my breakthrough! That was the word from the Lord I needed to hear. The last two verses especially arrested my troubled spirit, and peace came into my mind because I believed what I read: "I had fainted, unless I had believed to see the goodness of the LORD in the land of the living. Wait on the LORD: *be of good courage*, and he shall strengthen thine heart: wait, I say, on the LORD."

I remembered how I'd read "Be of good cheer" in John 16:33. Why be positive? Because Jesus said, "I have overcome the world." God, through Jesus, would strengthen my heart and fill me with hope. I believed that. And I believed then as I know today that He will do what He said He'll do!

Now, God didn't tell me that so I would sit back and wait on Him to fix the situation I was facing. *Waiting* doesn't mean "doing nothing." It means resting in the fact that God is handling things according to *His* good pleasure, and so we shouldn't worry about the issue. Anxiety should have no place in our lives while we're waiting on God. *Wait* means to "listen to the voice of God and do what He tells us to do with diligence and perseverance." Logic or reasoning has little play in waiting on the Lord because His ways are not always our ways (Isaiah 55:9). God is the sovereign Lord, and we need to (and want to!) give every thought and deed to Him. Waiting on Him means to move when He says move and to stand still when He says don't move. Waiting means to rejoice in the Lord always because He tells us to rejoice: "In everything give thanks; for this is the will of God in Christ Jesus for you" (1 Thessalonians 5:18).

With this encouragement from the heart of God, I traded my constant tears for the mind of God—and that led me to a life-changing discovery.

Why Didn't Somebody Tell Me?

After reading Psalm 27 and getting such relief, I started to really study my Bible. Before each reading, I prayed for God to open the eyes of my understanding because I wanted to know the truth.

Someone gave me a Ryrie Study Bible, and as I was previewing it one day, I noticed a study in the back called "The Doctrine of Demons." *What?* I certainly didn't hear much talk about demons because people talking about them were generally considered off their rockers. I wondered, *Are demons real? Or do people try to scare us into living straight by spooking us with the idea of demons?* First I looked up what a *doctrine* is. From the Latin *doctrina*, it means "a code of beliefs," "a body of teachings or instructions," "taught principles or positions." Then I looked up what demons are. Here's what I learned:

> So what are demons? What kind of creatures are they? What is their origin?
>
> We describe demons as disembodied spirit beings that have an intense craving to occupy physical bodies. Their first choice is a human body, but rather than remain in a disembodied condition, they are willing to enter even a body of an animal (Luke 8:32-33).
>
> Even though demons have no bodies, they have all the normally accepted marks of personality:
>
>> *Will*—"I will return to my house from which I came" (Matthew 12:44). The demon exercises its will to make a decision, and then follows it up with the action.
>>
>> *Emotion*—"Even the demons believe—and tremble" (James 2:19). This is outward manifestation of the fear of the demon inside.
>>
>> *Intellect*—More than one year before the disciples began to realize who they were following, the demon in this passage told Jesus, "I know who you are—the Holy One of God" (Mark 1:24).
>>
>> *Self-awareness*—"My name is Legion; for we are many" (Mark 5:9). The demon was aware of its own identity and that of the other demons occupying the man.

Ability to speak—In the Gospels and in Acts there are many examples of demons speaking through the vocal organs of a person.

The Greek word for demon is *diamonion* and is derived from a primary word, *daimon*. Greek mythology depicts two main orders of "gods" who dwell in the "heavenlies." The higher order is called *theos*, perhaps celestial beings (plural *theoi*). The lower order is called *daimon*...One special function of the *daimons* was to assign to each human being the destiny appointed for him/her by the *theoi*—the gods on the highest level.

On a lower earthly (terrestrial) level are the *daimonions* (demons). They are dominated and directed by the "gods" on a higher level. Possibly the *theoi* direct the *daimons* who in turn direct the *daimonions*.

Demons manifest themselves through humanity under many different names. Scripture speaks of lying spirits (1 Kings 22:23), a spirit of dizziness (Isaiah 19:14), a spirit of prostitution (Hosea 5:4), a deaf and mute spirit (Mark 9:25), a spirit of fear (Romans 8:15), a spirit of stupor (Romans 11:8), a spirit of timidity (2 Timothy 1:7), a spirit of falsehood (1 John 4:6), and so on. These are possible examples of afflicting spirits, and there are many other ways in which evil spirits can afflict people.

Please understand that we are not speaking of demon possession; we are talking about demonic affliction. Demons do not "possess" anything, especially human beings, because possession means ownership, and they do not own anything or anyone. The English word "possessed" is not the best translation from the original Greek, but unfortunately this is the term that has been used in many versions of the Bible. A better word is "demonized," which covers the range from mild afflictions to partial control of the person by evil spirits. Christians can be demonized both from within and without.

Christians can come under partial control of demonic forces
through such things as taking part in occultic activities.[1]

Once I learned what demons are, my curiosity got the best of
me. I spent hours studying my Bible and getting acquainted with
this side of the supernatural that I'd never been exposed to. I had
enough sense to realize that this study would put me in a different
mindset than that of my family and friends, and so I kept it to myself
for fear of being branded as too religious, a fanatic holy roller, or any
of the other monikers people lay on someone when they're uncomfortable with what a person is doing. In fact, I'm revealing publicly
my belief in the existence of demons for the first time in this book.
I've gone through so much stuff since the 1970s that now I'm comfortable with who I am and what I believe. And I want you to get
delivered and relieved like I am so you too can understand how to
fight and win against the wiles of the devil.

In my study, eventually I wondered, *People knew about this. Why
didn't they tell me about it earlier?* Perhaps they didn't for the same
reason I didn't tell anybody: fear of criticism. Are you afraid like
I was? That's fine. Just continue to study this issue for yourself so
you'll know what God says about demons and how to win.

Warning! The enemy has come to steal, kill, and destroy. Satan
does not want you to consciously know about his dirty work. Before
you study it, *pray.* Cover yourself with the blood of Jesus to protect
yourself from the schemes of the devil. Otherwise you'll become
vulnerable to his wiles and he'll be working on you because he
knows his evil schemes are going to be revealed.

Demonic Manifestations

I haven't done in-depth research into the categories and work
of demons, but the following list provides a basic framework of possible demonic activity.[2]

Possible Demonic Activity
and Influence

Note: With our God-given free will, we sometimes choose to "give in" to fleshly pursuits, such as sexual sins, overeating, and selfishness. Sometimes it's difficult to tell what may be demonic activity and what may be fleshly pursuits in our "natural man" natures. And sometimes our "occasional" sins become habitual lifestyles, and that often means our fleshly desires are being intensified and augmented by demonic whispers and encouragement. Regardless of the source, when we become aware of our sins, we need to repent, ask God for forgiveness and help, and turn from them.

Addictions/Dependencies/Overemphasis

* alcohol	* romantic fantasies
* caffeine	* sports
* compulsions (eating, gambling, gluttony, etc.)	* sugar
* drugs (prescription and nonprescription)	* television
* overindulgence	* video games

Anger

* bitterness	* hate
* child abuse	* malice
* cruelty	* physical, mental, emotional abuse
* denigrating self and others	* rage
* destructiveness	* retaliation
* fighting	* strife

Bitterness

* backbiting	* holding grudges
* coldness	* inability to love
* complaining	* refusing reconciliation
* feeling tormented	* resentment

* scoffing/derision	* ungratefulness
* unforgiveness	* without pity

Compulsive Behavior/Bondages

* addictions/cravings	* feeling lost, not belonging
* difficulty in being still	* feeling trapped and broken
* difficulty listening	* inability to trust
* dissatisfaction	* lack of self-control
* doubting salvation	* obsessed with ideas, projects, rituals
* driving others or self	* self-destruction
* eating disorders	* self-indulgence
* false guilt and burdens	* spiritual blindness
* fears	* unhealthy relationships and associations

Controlling

* aggressiveness	* manipulation
* appeasement	* nagging
* domineering (male and female)	* possessiveness
* denial	* pride

Dishonesty

* cheating	* low self-image
* compromise	* lying
* deceit	* scheming
* double-crossing	* self-delusion
* exaggeration	* shiftiness
* false compassion	* sneakiness
* false spirituality	* trickery
* false teaching	* unfairness
* flattery	* unscrupulousness
* hypocrisy	

Escape

* addictions/cravings	* forgetfulness
* excessive sleep	* lack of alertness
* fantasies	* passivity

Fears

* attraction to macabre	* fear of not being loved or liked
* claustrophobia	* fear of persecution
* confusion	* fear of poverty
* cowardice	* fear of responsibility
* dislike of being alone	* fear of sexual inadequacy
* dread	* fear of sexual perversion
* embarrassment	* feeling incapacitated
* excessive caution	* fretfulness
* excessive self-awareness	* hypochondria
* excessive sensitivity	* hysteria
* faithlessness	* inability to call upon God
* fear of abandonment	* inability to find peace
* fear of accusation	* inability to relax
* fear of authorities	* inadequacy
* fear of being a victim	* intimidation
* fear of being exposed	* nervousness and nervous habits
* fear of being wrong	* obsessed with death
* fear of condemnation	* panic attacks
* fear of confrontation	* paranoia
* fear of darkness	* phobias
* fear of failure	* reclusiveness
* fear of illness	* superstition
* fear of judgment	

Hindrances

* always studying but never understanding the truth of Christ	* difficulty staying awake when hearing or reading God's Word
* basing salvation on personal worthiness	* disappointment with God
* being ashamed of Christ	* discomfort in Christian settings
* being hardened to the truth	* dislike of yourself and how God made you
* believing and promoting false doctrines and religions	* disrupting Christian teachings and meetings
* believing God doesn't want you	* distracted from spiritual things
* believing God's commands are harsh and difficult	* feeling God is apathetic or vindictive
* bitterness toward God	* inability to trust God
* blaming God	* inability to understand God's Word
* blasphemy	* not believing God or His miracles
* boredom	* not loving the truth
* critical spirit	* religious frenzies
* denying Jesus (deity, blood atonement, as Messiah)	* twisting or misinterpreting God's Word
* deriding Christians	* wanting to be or become God

Judgmental/Legalism

* accusatory	* gossip, sharing and listening
* blaming others	* imposing impossible standards on self and others
* condemnation	* inflexibility
* contempt	* lack of compassion
* critical spirit to self and others	* ridicule
* fault-finding	* sarcasm
* feeling guilty for expressing feelings	* self-judgment
* feeling others' actions are never good enough	* stoicism

Lack of Love

* abusiveness	* lack of mercy
* belligerence	* masochism
* disloyalty	* partiality
* failure to discipline children	* provoking children to anger
* failure to love unconditionally	* reviling
* hatefulness	* rudeness
* husband failing to love wife as Christ loves the church	* sadism
* indifference	* slander
* insensitivity	* wife refusing to honor husband

Occult

* astral projection	* Ouija and other divination methods
* astrology	* pagan religions
* automatic handwriting	* palmistry
* black or white magic	* past life readings
* casting spells or hexes	* psychic healing
* channeling	* reading tea leaves
* clairvoyance	* ritualism
* conjuring	* Satanism
* consulting the dead	* sorcery
* crystal ball	* spiritism
* divination	* superstition
* fetishes	* tarot cards
* fortune-telling	* transcendental meditation
* horoscopes	* use of mediums
* hypnosis	* voodoo
* mind control	* yoga
* mind reading	

Pride

* agitation	* insolence
* argumentativeness	* intolerance
* arrogance	* irritability
* being dictatorial	* perfectionism
* being overbearing	* prejudice or bigotry
* boastfulness	* pride of accomplishments
* condescending	* pride of appearance
* contentious	* pride of possessions
* criticalness	* rejection of God
* egocentricity	* scorn
* excessive competitiveness	* selfish ambition
* false humility	* selfishness
* impatience	* self-justification
* insistence on having your own way	* stubbornness

Psychological Issues

* apathy	* emotionalism
* brokenness	* false guilt
* chaotic living environment	* feeling oppressed
* condemnation	* feeling suppressed
* confusion	* feeling you should be punished
* defeatism	* having a blank mind
* dejection	* hearing noises and voices
* depression	* hopelessness
* despair	* hysteria
* discontent	* impulsiveness
* discouragement	* inability to concentrate
* disgust	* inability to control thinking
* dissatisfaction	* inability to cope
* double-mindedness	* inability to cry
* eccentricities of speech (annoying, repetitious, affected)	* incoherence

* indecisiveness	* recklessness
* insanity	* self-absorption
* insecurity	* self-deceit
* irrationality	* self-destructive fantasies and/or tendencies
* listlessness	* self-pity
* negativity	* sense of failure
* obsession with misery	* severe mood swings
* obsessive introspection	* shame
* obsessive rituals to control surroundings	* unreasonable expectations
* oversensitivity	* unreasonableness
* paralysis of the will	* withdrawal
* powerlessness in Christian life	* wounded spirit

Rebellion

* dishonoring parents	* quarreling
* dishonoring spouse	* refusal to submit
* fighting	* self-will
* independence from God	* stubbornness
* insubordination	* undermining others
* obstinacy	* willfulness
* pouting	

Rejection

* abandonment	* feeling others are persecuting you
* caring too much what others think	* feeling rejected
* comparing yourself with others	* feeling others are unfair to you
* failure to feel loved	* feeling you can't be forgiven by God
* fear of witnessing	* feeling you don't belong
* feeling God can't use you	* feeling you're the victim
* feeling inadequate	* isolation

* letting people take advantage of you	* self-rejection
* martyr complex	* shame over physical appearance
* mistrust for and by others	* tendency to withdraw from others
* refusal or inability to express love	* unreasonable expectations
* self-condemnation	* unworthiness

Sexual Sins

* abnormal sexual desire	* lustful fantasies
* abortion	* masochism
* adulterous fantasies	* necrophilia
* adultery	* nymphomania
* bestiality	* obsession with sex
* body defilement	* orgies
* child molestation	* pedophilia
* coarse jesting	* pornography
* degrading God-given sexual drive	* premarital sex
* exhibitionism	* promiscuity
* fornication	* prostitution
* frigidity	* rape
* guilt from sexual misbehavior	* sadomasochism
* homosexuality	* sexual abuse
* immorality	* sodomy
* impurity	* transvestitism
* incest	* unfaithfulness to spouse
* inordinate passion	* voyeurism
* lesbianism	* withholding sex from spouse
* licentiousness	

Stealing/Greed

* covetousness	* material lust
* irresponsible spending	* never satisfied
* kleptomania	* rationalization
* lack of conscience	* stinginess
* love of money and possessions	

Unbelief

* distrust	* pessimism
* doubt	* rationalism
* hardness of heart	* skepticism
* idolatry	* suspicion

Worldliness

* being profane in mind and speech	* empty and worldly chatter
* boredom	* entanglement in worldly affairs
* cursing	* hedonism
* dabbling in paranormal activities	* materialism

If the long list on that chart is even partway true, we encounter demons or their activities every day. When we want to be good and holy, there's always something to entice us to be the opposite.

Unfortunately, when life is happening around us, who can walk around every minute of every day concentrating on the Lord? Frankly, if you're like me, some of the simplest things sidetrack us. Somebody asking me the same question I answered five minutes earlier is sure to shift my focus.

The Possible Demonic Activity and Influence list isn't talking about the once-in-a-while slip-ups we all make. It's referring to these activities *when they become a lifestyle*. If you're fighting every day to keep from lying, and you struggle against being a perpetual and habitual liar, you may be battling a demon spirit of lying. It's so easy to succumb. We all have to be careful about giving in to occasional lying. The more we do it, the easier it is to develop the habit. Eventually we yield to the influence of a demon spirit and lying becomes a way of life.

But please know I'm not saying that everything negative in our lives or every time we choose to do something suspect there's a demon at work. God gave us the ability to make choices...and we don't always choose wisely. But we need to know what we're up against and prepare ourselves to fight and win.

Don't be afraid. The Lord of lords and King of kings is your refuge and strength. Jesus is your salvation:

> The LORD also will be a refuge for the oppressed,
> A refuge in times of trouble.
> And those who know Your name will put their trust in You;
> For You, LORD, have not forsaken those who seek You (Psalm 9:9-10).

Learning Spiritual Warfare

My study about demons led me to the study of angels. Since then I've studied the doctrine of God, the doctrine of Jesus Christ, the doctrine of the Holy Spirit, and much more. Each study brings me closer into the holy realm of God through Jesus Christ. It's so exciting! The more I know, the more I know what I don't know, and the more I want to learn.

There are some things God cannot or will not do. He won't lie or go back on His word. He won't fail to keep His promises. He won't disrespect the Godhead (the Trinity—the Father, Son, and Holy Spirit) or disappoint us. He stays true to His teachings and won't tell us to do something against His Word or retract our firm foundation of salvation through Jesus. (That's an *Amen!*)

One of the most beneficial results from all this study is a greater knowledge of spiritual warfare. I now know what it is, how it affects me and others, and what to do about it to win. I had to nearly have a nervous breakdown before I discovered the blessing of knowing what our daily battles are all about. As somebody expressed it, "There's a messing before a blessing!" That's a shame, but it's often so true. We learn very little when things are going well. It's when things are at their worst that we finally yield our arrogance and pride to the only One who can do our helpless souls any good—God, our heavenly Father. Because there's a blessing in the messing, keep on trusting God and praising His name. He's truly in control!

The feeling of nearly losing my mind over the stress and tension of my life didn't go away immediately. I still had periods of discontentment and unsettlement because my problems were not resolved. But my reactions to the situation changed from anxiety to adjustment and from anger to acknowledgment. The knowledge I gained helped me look more closely at me, my surroundings, my family and friends, and at things that might attract demon spirits. If these spirits were alive and intelligent and had those qualities I learned about, they were something to reckon with. I didn't want to *invite* them into my life. And I didn't want them to "get in" through somebody or something in my possession.

I got so serious about eradicating any potential demon danger in my life that I arranged for a seminar about cleaning out the demons in your surroundings. I opened my home and invited my closest friends to learn what I was discovering. I was surprised to find out how much stuff I'd allowed in my presence and surroundings that *could* (note I'm not saying *did*) attract demons.

My mind was sparked to know more about what to suspect as demon "inviters" when I read *Pigs in the Parlor* by Frank and Ida Mae Hammond. They teach about demon spirits and how we let them into our homes without knowing it. Based on the authors' experiences with the supernatural, they list these as some things that can attract demons, depending on what they've been used for or what has been attributed to them:

- books and objects identified with anything related to Satan's kingdom
- masks and other objects that have to do with witches
- artifacts and objects from fetish activities and other religions

- creatures of the dark, such as owls, bats, and frogs
- sinful activities on the part of a former or current resident[3]

The words of God in Deuteronomy 7:25-27 come to mind:

> You shall burn the carved images of their gods with fire; you shall not covet the silver or gold that is on them, nor take it for yourselves, lest you be snared by it; for it is an abomination to the LORD your God. Nor shall you bring an abomination into your house, lest you be doomed to destruction like it. You shall utterly detest it and utterly abhor it, for it is an accursed thing.

Time for Removal and Destruction

I'll never forget the call I got from one of my best friends one evening. It went something like this:

> Thelma, something's going on in my house. It's happened before and I ignored it, but it's happening again. The draperies on my wall are swaying back and forth like a fan is blowing on them. But the windows aren't open, and there are no air vents near them. And even if there were, it's too cool to have the air conditioning on.
>
> It's spooky because I can't understand what's happening. I was just sitting on the bed when the draperies started moving back and forth, swaying like somebody was moving them.
>
> I'm scared. Something weird is going on here. Can you come over so you can see what I'm talking about, and so I won't think I'm losing my mind?

I went to her house and immediately noticed again some items that gave me the creeps every time I went over there. She was a collector of items from several islands where her husband lived before they got married. I asked her if she knew what they meant and who had made them. She didn't know the answer to either question. They were just objects obtained when she visited there.

We stood in her house and prayed that God would give us the discernment to know what to discard and what to keep if necessary. As we prayed, we walked around her house. A number of items were brought to mind to be destroyed. They were not to be given away to someone else but were to be burned or broken to prevent anyone else from experiencing demon activity. My friend had paid a lot for some of these items, but her safety and contentment were far more important than holding on to objects that invited demons in.

When we finished praying and getting rid of the items, peace came upon both of us. We realized we'd been obedient in ridding her house of demon attractors. She confessed that she'd known it was demonic activity in her house because this wasn't the first weird experience she'd had.

Since that time there have been other demon attempts to be active there, so she and I continue to pray for sharpness in our discernment as we spiritually clean out anything that might welcome the spirits of evil and might hinder the flow of God in her home and the lives of her family. We do the same for my home and family. When I feel an oppression in the house, perhaps from visitors or negative issues, or something, I go through my house and ask Jesus to take care of any enemies lurking about. I also pray that God will show me what I need to do.

I'm not having a breakdown now; I'm having a buildup! I'm calling on Jesus and then standing up to the enemy of our souls. I say to the devil, "In the name of Jesus, the Lord rebuke you and destroy you for His name's sake. Amen."

A picture is like a thousand words, and a live demonstration puts you in the middle of the performance. I was there. I saw for myself what was happening when I went to my friend's house. Yes, it was weird, but the Word of God spoken in prayer by His children won over evil.

Are you convinced yet? Are you ready to enter the battle? Or do you need to get a clearer picture of what spiritual warfare is?

We're going to go into this in more detail, but first I want you to know I had to be broken, to experience a breakdown, before I was ready to recognize the blessing of understanding what I was fighting against. The problem wasn't my circumstances; it was the enemy—Satan—trying to steal my contentment, kill my joy, and destroy my life and the lives of my loved ones.

At the time of my tribulation nobody I knew told me what was happening…or maybe they were afraid to tell me because they weren't sure I'd believe them. But I'm not afraid to tell you! You're fighting an enemy much more ferocious than you can imagine. But he is powerless when you know how to fight him and who to call upon for help.

Ain't that good news!

4

Weeds in the Garden

Let me tell you about one of my biggest battles (I even wrote about it in a magazine article). It reminds me of our everyday fight against the things that can choke and smother us. This battle wasn't spiritual, physical, or mental. It was external. At first it appeared like a never-ending battle that was provoking, annoying, and disgusting me at every turn. I had never had such a struggle before.

My husband and I purchased land in the most beautiful countryside we ever saw. We knew God resided there because the sky was bluer, the grass greener, and the air fresher than we'd experienced before. We were excited about this modest country home we'd build for rest and relaxation. Little did I know that at times this place would be a source of great exasperation.

Our battle centered on weeds.

I'd never seen or heard of weeds so stubborn they couldn't be pulled up, killed by spray, or covered up without returning to reseed.

We had experts come out to show us the secrets of weed control. We spent major money on liquid poison that would kill the weeds, not knowing that instead what it would kill was the grass we'd planted three times. The weeds were stubborn, overbearing, and growing out of control.

Flowers in the Weeds

Meanwhile, among these weeds I planted four crepe myrtle trees. When I bought those trees they were skinny, had very little foliage, and needed special watering for three weeks. I purchased four varieties of crepe myrtles because I'd seen them all over the country-side and fell in love with their luscious red buds, regal lavender blossoms, gorgeous white cascades, and romantic pink bouquets. Their blooms added the most beautiful colors to gardens, walkways, hillsides, and landscapes all around us. When I planted the trees I believed that one day they would also grace the yard with majestic colors.

I planted them in the spring. I watered and watched them care-fully for one year without any visible sign of growth. I was con-cerned because they looked like they hadn't grown at all. Plus they were surrounded by the ever-persistent weeds. I knew I'd done everything I could possibly do to help them grow. I'd planted them in the correct soil and watered them often. But my heart failed as I waited and waited and waited for them to grow and bloom.

Then one day as I walked outside, disgusted again about the weeds and wondering what in the world to do about them, I noticed a few tiny round buds peeking out on the top of some of the crepe myrtle branches. *Wow! Maybe we'll have a few flowers this year after all!* I thought.

Three weeks passed and the buds increased and finally, to my surprise—shazam!—there were luscious, strong, hardy, vibrant blossoms that woke up my spirit and caused me to holler, "Thank You, Lord! Thank You for the beauty of the earth. Oh, how great Thou art!"

Earlier, with my limited human vision, I couldn't see any signs of growth, yet God was working all the time. At the right time, in the proper season, in spite of the infestation of weeds, the crepe myrtles produced what they were created to do—beautiful splendor.

Today, as you look at your life, you may see a mass of weeds that seem impossible to exterminate. Do you see weeds of discontent, lack of peace, poverty, financial devastation, heartbreak, heartache, indecision, abandonment, disappointment, family upheaval, broken relationships, grief, or pain? There is one thing I've found that holds me in the ground and waters my roots and nurtures the branches of my heart: It's *faith* in God.

More Faith

The disciples once said to the Lord Jesus, "We need more faith; tell us how to get it." Jesus answered, "If your faith were only the size of a mustard seed, it would be large enough to uproot that mulberry tree over there and send it hurtling into the sea! Your command would bring immediate results!" (Luke 17:5-6 TLB).

What was Jesus saying? A planted mustard seed is small but hardy, alive, and growing. Watch as it grows and see it blossom, going from the tiniest seed to a massive, great, strong, and useful plant. The seed is almost invisible at first, but underneath the soil it goes through an imperceptible change that produces major results that will uproot and destroy the competing weeds surrounding it.

When you look at your faith, the size isn't nearly as important as the quality.

God gives every believer a measure of faith. In that faith we can...

- follow God despite difficulties
- believe in something when we can't see the end results
- know in our hearts that God is going to keep His promises, whether now or later

- realize the things God *cannot* or will not do—He won't lie, He won't abandon His Word, He won't fail, He won't love you too much, He won't stop holding the world in His hands, He won't yield to temptation, and He won't go back on His promises to us

So as you combat the weeds in your life, remember God is the God of weeds. When all else fails, He'll either pluck up the weeds for you or give you a beautiful tree in their midst to reveal His love, glory, grace, and faithfulness. Just watch! He'll keep His promises. For He can do abundantly above all that we can ask or even imagine.

At the beginning of mankind, when Adam and Eve were in the Garden of Eden, there were no weeds. The garden was perfect. There were no sticker buds, crab grass, dandelions—nothing that would cause harm to the beautiful foliage or to people. There were no pests. It was utopia, the perfect world. I can just imagine Adam and Eve walking in the morning dew, getting their feet damp from the mist that came up from the earth to keep the foliage watered. In my mind's eye I can see them holding hands as they stroll among the animals who are dashing and dancing and playing. Yes, I see the wolf with the lamb, the gazelle with the monkeys, the antelope with the alligators, the great big elephant with the little-bitty frog—all having a marvelous time with nothing to fear.

They had no idea there was a predator in the garden. They didn't even know what a predator was. They'd never heard of one. Again, in my mind, I see the two-legged creature that hadn't yet revealed his true nature. He was going around making gorgeous music, serenading the man and woman, pleasing the flying birds and the floating fish and the frolicking animals, charming everyone, and seemingly adding to the general pleasure. This predator was named Lucifer, son of the morning. We know more about him now, thanks to what the Lord revealed through the prophet Isaiah:

How you are fallen from heaven,
O Lucifer, son of the morning!
How you are cut down to the ground,
You who weakened the nations!
For you have said in your heart:
"I will ascend into heaven,
I will exalt my throne above the stars of God;
I will also sit on the mount of the congregation
On the farthest sides of the north;
I will ascend above the heights of the clouds,
I will be like the Most High."
Yet you shall be brought down to Sheol,
To the lowest depths of the Pit (Isaiah 14:12-15).

The Greatest Fallen Angel

Lucifer was made with instruments of music in his body. The workmanship of his timbrels and pipes was prepared for him on the day he was created. He was an archangel set apart from the cherubim and seraphim in position and authority. He was the number four created being in the kingdom of heaven. Look at how the prophet Ezekiel describes him through these words spoken to Lucifer by God:

You were the seal of perfection,
Full of wisdom and perfect in beauty.
You were in Eden, the garden of God;
Every precious stone was your covering:
The sardius, topaz, and diamond,
Beryl, onyx, and jasper,
Sapphire, turquoise, and emerald with gold.
The workmanship of your timbrels and pipes
Was prepared for you on the day you were created.

You were the anointed cherub who covers;
I established you;

You were on the holy mountain of God;
You walked back and forth in the midst of fiery stones.
You were perfect in your ways from the day you were created,
Till iniquity was found in you.

By the abundance of your trading
You became filled with violence within,
And you sinned;
Therefore I cast you as a profane thing
Out of the mountain of God;
And I destroyed you, O covering cherub,
From the midst of the fiery stones.

Your heart was lifted up because of your beauty;
You corrupted your wisdom for the sake of your splendor;
I cast you to the ground,
I laid you before kings,
That they might gaze at you.

You defiled your sanctuaries
By the multitude of your iniquities,
By the iniquity of your trading;
Therefore I brought fire from your midst;
It devoured you,
And I turned you to ashes upon the earth
In the sight of all who saw you (Ezekiel 28:12-18).

With all this good stuff going on with Lucifer, who would suspect him of being a predator? The birds and the bees and the flowers and the trees wouldn't have known. And the human beings in the garden didn't know what a predator was either. They were too busy enjoying themselves to pay any attention. They were busy doing what God commanded them to do:

> Then God blessed them, and God said to them, "Be fruit-
> ful and multiply; fill the earth and subdue it; have dominion

over the fish of the sea, over the birds of the air, and over every living thing that moves on the earth."

And God said, "See, I have given you every herb that yields seed which is on the face of all the earth, and every tree whose fruit yields seed; to you it shall be for food. Also, to every beast of the earth, to every bird of the air, and to everything that creeps on the earth, in which there is life, I have given every green herb for food"; and it was so (Genesis 1:28-30).

God wanted Adam and Eve to use their vast resources in the service of Him and people and to have dominion (ruling power, authority, control) over everything He had made on earth. Human beings are the only creatures who received from God this ability, responsibility, and authority.

Because they didn't recognize there was a predator lurking in their midst who was different from the rest of creation, it's possible that Adam and Eve, completely honest and vulnerable, became friends with the devil. Perhaps they walked and talked and had the fellowship of friendship with him for some time. They trusted him.

Perhaps they discussed with him the wonders of the forbidden tree many times. Can't you imagine them wondering, *What would really happen if we touched it?* Wouldn't you be curious of the powers of a tree that you were told to have nothing to do with? Don't you think your curiosity would be aroused?

Are you wondering why God didn't warn Adam and Eve about Lucifer? Me too. That's one of the biblical mysteries we, in our humanness, don't understand or don't have all the details of. Suffice it to say that God was protecting them by asking them to obey Him.

You and I know about bad things, but Eve had never encountered their manifestation. All Eve knew was that she and Adam were not to have any touchie-feelie-eatie relationship with this tree of the knowledge of good and evil. How was she to know that Lucifer, her so-called friend, had started an insurrection that caused a great war in heaven, resulting in God expelling this beautiful angel out of His heavenly home and casting him down to earth?

> And there was war in heaven. Michael and his angels fought against the dragon, and the dragon and his angels fought back. But he was not strong enough, and they lost their place in heaven. The great dragon was hurled down—that ancient serpent called the devil, or Satan, who leads the whole world astray. He was hurled to the earth, and his angels with him (Revelation 12:7-9 NIV).

Although some of this scenario is pure conjecture based on limited information, we do know the basics—that the serpent was in the garden.

Falling into the Trap

One day when Eve was open to suggestion and curious in mind, the cunning and calculating devil—the enemy Lucifer, who was now called Satan—came to feed her human desires with embellished information. He added fictitious details to the truth God had shared and thus aroused her impulses and tantalized her pride.

She fell into the trap of temptation and desire that you and I are warned about in the New Testament: "But each one is tempted when, by his own evil desire, he is dragged away and enticed. Then, after desire has conceived, it gives birth to sin; and sin, when it is full-grown, gives birth to death" (James 1:14-15 NIV).

The evil devil tempted Eve. She disobeyed God and ate of the forbidden fruit from the only tree in the garden that Adam was told not to touch. (God or Adam must have told Eve about not eating the fruit.) And Adam, being so much in love with Eve and impulsive himself, disobeyed God too. He also fell prey to the embellished conversation of Satan concerning the power of the tree of the knowledge of good and evil shared by Eve. He ate of the fruit. Eve and Adam made their choices. They chose to disobey God.

After their choices were made and their sin committed, weeds began to grow in the garden of their lives. They were cast out of the perfect garden into a world of sin, a world of evil perpetrated by Satan and craftily infesting the thoughts of mankind. Satan is the unholy god of this age and is the author of powers, principalities, authorities, wickedness, unrighteousness, and sin. Evil originates from Satan. And because of it, he is destined for the lake of fire during the final consummation of this present age on earth.

Adam and Eve's story had been absolutely beautiful and pristine before they sinned. Look at it again, with tragic recognition of all they lost:

> Then the LORD God took the man and put him in the garden of Eden to tend and keep it. And the LORD God commanded the man, saying, "Of every tree of the garden you may freely eat; but of the tree of the knowledge of good and evil you shall not eat, for in the day that you eat of it you shall surely die."
>
> And the LORD God said, "It is not good that man should be alone; I will make him a helper comparable to him." Out of the ground the LORD God formed every beast of the field and every bird of the air, and brought them to Adam to see what he would call them. And whatever Adam called each living creature, that was its name. So Adam gave names to all cattle, to the birds of the air, and to every beast of the field. But for Adam there was not found a helper comparable to him.
>
> And the LORD God caused a deep sleep to fall on Adam, and he slept; and He took one of his ribs, and closed up the flesh in its place. Then the rib which the LORD God had taken from man He made into a woman, and He brought her to the man.
>
> And Adam said:
>
>> "This is now bone of my bones
>> And flesh of my flesh;

> She shall be called Woman,
> Because she was taken out of Man."

Therefore a man shall leave his father and mother and be joined to his wife, and they shall become one flesh.

And they were both naked, the man and his wife, and were not ashamed (Genesis 2:15-25).

Then came the tragic choices Adam and Eve made, and their paradise was lost.

Like nuisances, the weeds of sin sprang up in the lives of the first biblical people. They would pass on this heritage of sinfulness to all of humanity that followed. The world now sees the horror of the infestation of satanic plants that literally choke the lives out of millions and billions of people. These are sin weeds that have become fire hazards—vegetation that is not only noxious but also dangerous and deadly. Sin grasses, stubble, brush, tumbleweeds... clippings and cuttings that endanger our health and safety by sustaining and providing shelter for an invasion of demons. They are unwanted, but they attach themselves to us and our environment anyway.

Getting Serious About Warfare

The weeds of sin are abundant all around us. That's why we need to understand what we're fighting against every minute of every day—and we must be prepared for battle so we won't get discouraged and give in. Remember—God wants us to win!

Satan is our enemy; demons are our enemies. They're the fallen angels who followed Lucifer (Satan) from heaven when he was expelled, and they hate Christians. They're fighting us today, trying to win followers for their evil leader. We're dealing with spiritual warfare day in and day out. The only way we can fight and win is to know what the Word of God tells us:

Finally, my brethren, be strong in the Lord and in the power of His might. Put on the whole armor of God, that you may be able to stand against the wiles of the devil. For we do not wrestle against flesh and blood, but against principalities, against powers, against the rulers of the darkness of this age, against spiritual hosts of wickedness in the heavenly places. Therefore take up the whole armor of God, that you may be able to withstand in the evil day, and having done all, to stand.

Stand therefore, having girded your waist with truth, having put on the breastplate of righteousness, and having shod your feet with the preparation of the gospel of peace; above all, taking the shield of faith with which you will be able to quench all the fiery darts of the wicked one. And take the helmet of salvation, and the sword of the Spirit, which is the word of God; praying always with all prayer and supplication in the Spirit, being watchful to this end with all perseverance and supplication for all the saints (Ephesians 6:10-18).

Though we walk in the flesh, we do not war according to the flesh. For the weapons of our warfare are not carnal but mighty in God for pulling down strongholds (2 Corinthians 10:3-4).

We are in the throes of spiritual warfare every second of every minute, of every hour, of every week, of every month, of every year, of every decade from point B (birth) to point D (death).

When we speak of spiritual warfare, what comes to mind? It may not be what you think because people have different ideas. Dr. Ed Murphy writes in *The Handbook for Spiritual Warfare:*

Some speak of the struggle between good and evil. Others talk of the battle between right and wrong, or between light and darkness. Still others refer to the conflict between the positive forces which seek to preserve life and order in the universe and the negative forces which tend to disturb and even destroy life and order. From a biblical perspective, however, this dualism is revealed to be an on-going conflict waged on two fronts: God and His angelic kingdom confront Satan and his demonic kingdom, while the children of God contend with the children of Satan.[1]

I think of spiritual warfare in these ways (yes, I still have weeds on my mind):

- Spiritual warfare is like weeds that reproduce in many ways: sometimes through seeds, sometimes through root suckers that spread out, sometimes through parts of the plant that resprout.

- These weeds produce *many* seeds.

- They produce *small* seeds.

- The seeds have fancy ways of getting carried around (floating on air or water, sticking to animals, and so forth).

- If you pull these weeds, they break off and resprout.

- The roots or stems of these weeds form rhizomes or runners.

- These weeds are hardy generalists and can live almost anywhere.

- They grow fast.

- Their seeds may stay dormant in the soil for long periods and then sprout in abundance.

- The nuisance of these weeds is they don't go away until killed.

The weeds of sin and disobedience can kill us body, soul, and spirit. Satan tried to get Jesus to plant and nurture weeds after He was baptized and started His ministry. But after every ploy of the

devil to tempt Jesus to disobey God, Jesus said, "It is written..."
Read the story from Matthew 4:1-11:

> Then Jesus was led up by the Spirit into the wilderness
> to be tempted by the devil. And when He had fasted forty
> days and forty nights, afterward He was hungry. Now when
> the tempter came to Him, he said, "If You are the Son of
> God, command that these stones become bread."
>
> But He answered and said, "It is written, 'Man shall not
> live by bread alone, but by every word that proceeds from
> the mouth of God.'"
>
> Then the devil took Him up into the holy city, set Him
> on the pinnacle of the temple, and said to Him, "If You are
> the Son of God, throw Yourself down. For it is written: 'He
> shall give His angels charge over you,' and, 'In their hands
> they shall bear you up, Lest you dash your foot against a
> stone.'"
>
> Jesus said to him, "It is written again, 'You shall not
> tempt the LORD your God.'"
>
> Again, the devil took Him up on an exceedingly high
> mountain, and showed Him all the kingdoms of the world
> and their glory. And he said to Him, "All these things I will
> give You if You will fall down and worship me."
>
> Then Jesus said to him, "Away with you, Satan! For it is
> written, 'You shall worship the LORD your God, and Him only
> you shall serve.'"
>
> Then the devil left Him, and behold, angels came and
> ministered to Him."

Jesus had to fight against spiritual warfare, and so do we! I've
been fighting life now for more than sixty-five years. As a child I
had terrible nightmares, and my granddaddy advised me to pray and
recite the twenty-third psalm and the Lord's prayer. It worked, and
God took away my fear. As I go through life I win many battles, but
I do lose a few. God gave me His Word long ago to use to fight these
battles, but for a time I didn't realize what I was doing.

Shelter in the Storm

I mentioned before that God once had me read and memorize Psalm 27 as it related to a painful time I was going through. At the time I had no idea why He wanted me to learn that scripture, but I'm glad I was obedient enough not only to learn it for myself but also to have the person I was concerned about learn it as well. What a surprise when a couple of years ago my oldest granddaughter told me she had a dream in which God told her to memorize that same passage. Here is this wonderful psalm in the New King James Version:

The Lord is my light and my salvation;
Whom shall I fear?
The Lord is the strength of my life;
Of whom shall I be afraid?
When the wicked came against me
To eat up my flesh,
My enemies and foes,
They stumbled and fell.
Though an army may encamp against me,
My heart shall not fear;
Though war may rise against me,
In this I will be confident.
One thing I have desired of the Lord,
That will I seek:
That I may dwell in the house of the Lord
All the days of my life,
To behold the beauty of the Lord,
And to inquire in His temple.
For in the time of trouble
He shall hide me in His pavilion;
In the secret place of His tabernacle
He shall hide me;
He shall set me high upon a rock.
And now my head shall be lifted up above my enemies all
    around me;

Therefore I will offer sacrifices of joy in His tabernacle;
I will sing, yes, I will sing praises to the LORD.
Hear, O LORD, when I cry with my voice!
Have mercy also upon me, and answer me.
When You said, "Seek My face,"
My heart said to You, "Your face, LORD, I will seek."
Do not hide Your face from me;
Do not turn Your servant away in anger;
You have been my help;
Do not leave me nor forsake me,
O God of my salvation.
When my father and my mother forsake me,
Then the LORD will take care of me.
Teach me Your way, O LORD,
And lead me in a smooth path, because of my enemies.
Do not deliver me to the will of my adversaries;
For false witnesses have risen against me,
And such as breathe out violence.
I would have lost heart, unless I had believed
That I would see the goodness of the LORD
In the land of the living.
Wait on the LORD; be of good courage,
And He shall strengthen your heart;
Wait, I say, on the LORD!

I asked the Holy Spirit over and over to reveal to me why He had me reciting that scripture. Years before my granddaughter's dream, I attended a conference in Daytona Beach, Florida, that was sponsored by Pastors Michael and Francina Norman. One of the speakers at the conference told the story of her sister who was a victim of domestic violence. Every time she escaped from her husband and was in a safe place, they would connect again and she would go back to that kind of lifestyle. In spite of the warnings and safety provided her, there was a stronghold upon her mind that caused her to think she couldn't live without this abuser.

The sister told the story of God leading her to a certain scripture to give her consolation as she witnessed this horrible relationship continuing. The scripture was Psalm 27. She thought of it as the "abuse scripture for victims who want comfort." The sister was eventually murdered by her husband.

I was satisfied that I'd gotten my answer—that I needed to know Psalm 27 to combat trials. But what I was concerned about was a different kind of abuse. The person I was concerned about was in a stronghold of self-abuse. God wanted me to be a beacon of His Word and to infuse His Word into this person every chance I got. He also wanted me to know that as I watched this behavior become more and more severe, I was not to worry and become distraught because He would shine His light on the situation and take away my worry. And when the enemy of my soul tried to deter me, I had nothing to fear as long as I was confident that my relative and I were protected by the Lord.

Psalm 27 became my shelter in the time of a great storm. It also became a weapon of warfare that God gave me so that in every fight I could say I had the loving protection of the Lord. God was giving me an "it is written" to fight my inner feelings of doubt, fear, guilt, shame, anger, disgust, sadness, and despair. Even when I didn't really know why, I would recite this psalm and peace would come.

Then, recalling the magnitude of this scripture in my life, I got curious. I wondered how often my granddaughter needed to recall this passage. She's only a teenager, but teenagers are also fighting for their lives in a world of deception and evil.

I called and talked to my granddaughter and asked if she remembered the circumstances of her needing to learn this psalm. She answered yes. I asked her how often she used it and if there were any specific situations when she really needed it to fight and survive. Fortunately for her, she couldn't think of a specific incident where she needed it for survival. However, she admitted that she uses it a lot in her everyday circumstances. She uses it when she's worried about something. It comes in handy when she has words with a friend or someone's trying to misuse her or criticize her or talk about her wrongly. She said this scripture is her saving grace when she feels depressed or angry about something.

I thought, *What you're experiencing is just a preview of coming trials. God is preparing your mind so you can, like a computer, recall and select these words of comfort when the big tests come.* Yes, God is so concerned about us that He prepares us for battles even before we begin to fight. Hallelujah!

The Scripture I Needed Most

Along with Psalm 27, God directed me to another wonderful scripture—Philippians 4:6-7—that I live by all the time. I find myself drawing on these two scripture passages more than anyone else I know. I was drawn to these words from Philippians over a decade ago when I asked God to point out a scripture that would give me support in the coming year. I didn't know just how much I was going to need it until the first month of the year began with hurts and disappointments galore. Here's Philippians 4:6-7:

> Be anxious for nothing, but in everything by prayer and supplication, with thanksgiving, let your requests be made known to God; and the peace of God, which surpasses all understanding, will guard your hearts and minds through Christ Jesus.

When I first read this, I had a hard time getting past the "with thanksgiving" part. I didn't understand why I was supposed to give thanks for being in a predicament. But with prayer and study I discovered that "with thanksgiving" means to give thanks in everything because before the world began our sovereign God already worked out everything that concerns us. We don't have to figure life out. Our job is to trust Him.

Philippians 4:6-7 has brought me much ease and contentment. It has kept me from crying all night, getting an upset stomach, having bouts of depression, talking down or angrily to someone, and being impatient and out of control. Or, rather, it keeps me from these things when I *obey* what it says. The battle doesn't come until I get into some kind of situation and remember to pull this out of my mental database and use it to combat the negative forces in the situation.

Spiritual warfare is the battle for our minds. The devil deliberately attacks us using his demons. He wants to distract us from doing good, interfere with our righteous actions, demolish our godly relationships, dismantle our gifting, destroy the works of God's hands in our affairs, rearrange our holy desires, offend our witness as salt and light to the world and against evil, tarnish our good reputations, withhold our prosperity, ruin our health, strain our marriages, sabotage our ministries, disrespect our authorities, belittle our stand for right, defame our moral character, distort our honest business dealings, confuse our children, fracture our education, soil us with inappropriate legal matters, taint our friendly interactions, and overwhelm us so we tremble with fear.

Jesus is the answer for all the uncontrollable weeds of warfare in our lives! Realizing this, you don't have to give in! God wants you to win. So keep reading. It's time to get dressed for battle!

5

Rituals Untold

I've been keeping some secrets from you and my family. You're among the first to know. *Shhhh!* If you don't want to tell anybody else, you don't have to, but I think it's time I told on myself. First, let me define what *ritual* means to me so we'll be on the same page. A ritual for Thelma Wells means a regular, customary practice or reminder to keep me on track as I'm fighting the good fight of faith. It's something I do all or most of the time that reminds me how to be *ready to win* every day.

Most people who know me well are aware that one of my longstanding rituals is to have my entire family over for dinner every Sunday after church. Well, that's one ritual that hasn't been observed regularly since I was critically ill back in 2005. I don't have the stamina I used to have. And the grandkids are growing up and are involved in activities and friendships so they're not available every Sunday. But we do continue to get together as a family as often as we can.

We all have rituals. What are yours? Have you realized that even as we continue in rituals, they are sometimes modified out of necessity?

We also have rituals in our church services. Look at your Sunday programs. Your church probably follows the same order of worship Sunday after Sunday and has for years and years. We also have personal rituals. If you're like most of us, you usually get up at the same time; drink that coffee, juice, or water; and go about your daily routine doing some of the same things all the time. So, yes, everyone has rituals, whether acknowledged or not.

My Morning Rituals

When I started experiencing and ultimately studying spiritual warfare, I looked at the symbols of the Holy Spirit and decided to make some changes in my daily communication with the Lord. He and I had a good relationship, but I understood that it could be better.

The bathtub was a quiet place for me to pray and have communion with Jesus. So that's where He and I talked together often. That is, I would pray and then often be quiet so I could listen to what He had to say to me via my mind and spirit. The Holy Spirit's guidance and conviction is *awesome!* Now I want to sing again. There's an old hymn I relate to called "In the Garden." The refrain refreshes my spirit:

> And He walks with me,
> And He talks with me,
> And He tells me I am His own;
> And the joy we share as we tarry there,
> None other has ever known.[1]

Another of my morning rituals is singing. In the morning I don't want to listen to the news or hear any discussion except what will put me in mind to worship God and get in His presence. I often wake up with a praise song on my mind, and I often turn praise music on in my bedroom so I can listen to it as I'm preparing for the day. Even if I'm in a gloomy mood or easily annoyed by my to-do list for the day, listening to praise music has a soothing effect on my personality and thoughts. It gets me back to a positive frame of mind. In fact, I mostly keep praise or gospel music on in my house and car (and in my heart) all day every day. It sure helps me keep from losing my cool, and it keeps my mind on Jesus. Oh, now another song's on my mind. It's an old Negro spiritual:

> I woke up this morning with my mind stayed on Jesus.
> I woke up this morning with my mind stayed on Jesus.
> I woke up this morning with my mind stayed on Jesus.
> Hallelu [praise God!], Hallelu [thank You, Lord!], Hallelujah!
> I'm walking and talking with my mind stayed on Jesus.

Singing and praying are two parts of my daily ritual. I can break out in song any time of the day and at any point in a message when I'm speaking at a conference, teaching a class, or whatever. Music is a universal language that people all over the world relate to. We hear the tune to "Amazing Grace," and people in almost any language can join in the singing. Music is a common denominator among different religions, practices, ceremonies, celebrations, and rites.

Daily there's within my heart a melody that brings joy to my heart, a smile on my face, and peace to my mind. I sing to Jesus every day because that's a means of letting Him know I love Him. Oh yes, He knows that already, but I love to tell Him...just like I need to tell my husband how much I love him as often as I can. My husband knows I love him, but it sure makes him feel good when I say it. And it makes God feel good when we tell Him how much we love Him. In fact, when we praise Him and honor Him with our expressions of praise, He dances back over us with singing. It's true! God does rejoice over us:

The Lord your God in your midst,
The Mighty One, will save;
He will rejoice over you with gladness,
He will quiet you with His love,
He will rejoice over you with singing (Zephaniah 3:17).

Now that's something to shout about! Just think, the Almighty God of the universe, who made the heavens and the earth, hears me singing to Him and telling Him how I love Him. He watches me rejoice over His goodness to me. And then He turns around and shows His delight in me by singing over me and spinning like a top. If that's not love, I don't know what is! This two-way communication in song strengthens our relationship every time. I want to sing again!

There is a Name I love to hear,
I love to sing its worth;
It sounds like music in my ear,
The sweetest Name on earth.

Refrain
O how I love Jesus,
O how I love Jesus,
O how I love Jesus,
Because He first loved me!

It tells me of a Savior's love,
Who died to set me free;
It tells me of His precious blood,
The sinner's perfect plea.

It tells me of a Father's smile
Beaming upon His child;
It cheers me through this little while,
Through desert, waste, and wild.

It tells me what my Father hath
In store for every day,
And though I tread a darksome path,
Yields sunshine all the way.

It tells of One whose loving heart
Can feel my deepest woe;
Who in each sorrow bears
A part that none can bear below.

It bids my trembling heart rejoice.
It dries each rising tear.
It tells me, in a "still small voice,"
To trust and never fear.

Jesus, the Name I love so well,
The Name I love to hear:
No saint on earth its worth can tell,
No heart conceive how dear.

This Name shall shed its fragrance still
Along this thorny road,
Shall sweetly smooth the rugged hill
That leads me up to God.

And there with all the blood-bought throng,
From sin and sorrow free,
I'll sing the new eternal song
Of Jesus' love for me.[2]

An important part of my daily prayer is: "Lord, open the doors I need to walk through today, and close the doors I don't. Put people in my way I need to talk to today, and get people out of my way I don't. And please, Lord, don't let me waste time." I seem to get everything done I need to get done in a day's time. Not everything I want to do, but everything I need to do. And that's an amen!

So the secret's out on two of my rituals: I communicate with the Lord daily, and I sing to Him in the process.

Getting Properly Dressed

This next ritual might startle you a bit, but it's not mysterious or spooky. It's a routine I've developed to help me stay intent on the main focus in my life. It reminds me of Matthew 6:33, which tells me to seek first the kingdom of God and His righteousness, and everything good that God has for me will be granted to me. I started this procedure based on Ephesians 6:14-19 after I studied about the doctrine of angels and the doctrine of demons and the doctrine of the Holy Spirit. I want to stay focused on the One who lives in me spiritually by developing something practical that I can relate to every day. I want to remember that the Holy Spirit living in me is perfectly capable of keeping my mind focused and my heart clean, filling me with the truths of God's Word and helping me rejoice even when things aren't going the way I want them to when I keep in touch with Him. As part of my daily routine I get spiritually "dressed."

Dress for the Fight…

FIX YOUR HAIR

PAD YOUR BRA

TIGHTEN YOUR GIRDLE

PUT ON YOUR STOMPING SHOES

and get ready to win!

I think of it this way:

- *I fix my hair.* I put on the helmet of salvation.

- *I pad my bra (my heart).* I put on the breastplate of righteousness.

- *I tighten my girdle.* I put on the girdle (or belt) of truth.

- *I put on my stomping shoes.* I put on belief and praise.

- *I grab my shield and sword.* I declare my faith and trust in God. This also includes the sword of truth—God's Word.

Part of the way I "get dressed" is a bit unusual, but I've found it a very effective reminder of my purpose. I carry in my purse a little bottle of oil with frankincense and myrrh that I ask God to bless. There's no magic in the oil; oil is simply one of the symbols of the Holy Spirit. As I'm dressing physically to go about my day, I place a drop of oil on top of my head and say: "I'm covered with the helmet of salvation." That means I've accepted Christ as my personal Lord and Savior, and I've committed my life to serving Him.

I put a drop of oil on the center of my chest and say, "I'm covered by the breastplate of righteousness." Humanly speaking I am not pure in my heart, but because Jesus has accepted me as His child, He has purified my heart so I can't do anything wrong that His Holy Spirit won't convict me of and encourage me to repent. My heart is clean in the Spirit.

Then I cascade a tiny bit of oil around my waist and say, "I'm tightening the girdle of truth around me." When we know where the real truth about living comes from, we know that Jesus is the Way, the Truth, and the Life, and when we speak or think on this truth we have the support we need to make it through any circumstance.

I raise each foot, apply a drop of oil, and declare, "My feet are shod with the preparation of the gospel of peace." This means I know the good news of the Savior, and I'm eager to tell somebody about Him today.

After I do this, I'm covered from head to toe with the equipment to tackle and win any battle that comes my way that day—if I stay focused on Jesus.

But it doesn't stop there. I put oil in my hand and rub it as far as I can reach on my back and proclaim, "I'm wearing the shield of faith that covers my entire body because without faith it is impossible to please God." The shield of faith seals the deal.

The last item is putting the blessed oil on the palms of my hands. I decree that the Word of God (the Bible) is my sword to use to chase away anything the devil sends me today.

I'm ready then. I'm comforted that God's mercies are new every morning. Great is God's faithfulness! I can now go out and conquer the world, realizing that if God is for me, who can be against me? I'm cognizant of the fact that no weapon wielded against me can penetrate my armor. I can say assuredly that I trust in the Lord with all my heart, and I don't rely on my own understanding. In *all* my ways I acknowledge Him and allow Him to direct my paths (Proverbs 3:5-6).

Does this ritual make me perfect or make my day go by perfectly? No. There are interruptions, detours, distractions, and disagreements. But the Holy Spirit helps me focus on Christ, keeping me from going bad and hurting somebody's feelings most of the time. There are times when my flesh outweighs my righteousness. Part of our God-granted free will is that we make our own choices. During the day, when I take my mind off Jesus and start thinking about how I feel about a situation rather than about the One I know is working it out, I sometimes give in to poor choices and open the door for Satan to come into my life.

My Embattled Mind

I remember distinctly a day in May 2008 when my husband and I traveled to a speaking engagement in Texas, a couple of hours away from our house. About two hours before time for me to speak, I realized I'd left my "speaking clothes" hanging on the closet door at home. In more than thirty years of traveling and speaking, this had never happened to me. Urgency and stress raced through me. I found a department store and blew my monthly clothes budget by purchasing a three-piece outfit I had no matching shoes for. This was a little frustrating for me (I like to dress well when I represent my Savior). I counted my blessings though and was overjoyed the town had a store that carried clothing made by a designer I really liked. They had only one outfit that fit me and was appropriate for the occasion. (I only needed one.) I had to purchase shoes as well, and they were not cheap.

I was late for the dinner the hosts had prepared for George and me and nearly late getting to the church. I calmed down and prayed on my way, working my way back to focusing on the anointing of the Lord so my message would be authentically from Him and not from me. The Lord blessed the message, the people, and me.

Now, you would think I'd file this incident of forgetfulness in my mind's delete file and go on being thankful and relaxing. But I didn't. When I got into the car to go home, I kept thinking about it, although I didn't say anything about it to my husband. Non-essential stuff kept creeping into my mind: *What's happening to you? You act like you're losing your mind. You've never done such stupid stuff before. You pressed your clothes and hung them on the door so you could see them as you walked out of your bedroom, and yet you still walked off and left them. Are you getting that forgetful?*

I kept thinking.

Well, I am getting old, and maybe this is the first sign I'm getting mentally ill. I forgot something the other day—and now I can't even remember what it was. I'll be talking to people and forget what I was going to say. Oh my goodness! I must be getting senile or Alzheimer's or something. No, Lord! Please don't let me deteriorate like that.

I thought myself into a fearful frenzy but refused to share my dilemma for fear of seeming ungrateful for what God had done in the service. But not dealing with sin (not letting go and dwelling on me instead of all God had done) means it usually comes out another way.

A lovely friend and I had made plans for visiting with each other later that evening. She was from out of the city, and we wanted to spend a little time catching up. When she called, she made a statement about needing to keep another obligation and so we wouldn't be meeting. Then she called back with a question I thought was manipulative. With my mind already overloaded with nonsense and junk, I reacted to her comment with anger. I gave her a piece of my mind.

She was shocked; I was mad. I mean *really* mad! But as soon as I hung up the telephone, the Holy Spirit convicted me. I felt terrible about what I'd just done. This explosion was out of character for me. I was so rude and hateful over something that really didn't matter and that my friend had meant no harm about. Now my mind was burdened by the question of whether she could or would forgive me for the way I talked to her. I analyzed how I got to the point of responding to her in such an uncouth and hurtful way.

I'd given way for the devil to get into my mind and possibly destroy my relationship with this dear daughter in the Lord. It only takes a pin-sized hole for that old enemy to get in and sabotage good intentions and thought patterns. On the drive home, I'd worried about a journey toward mental illness. I'd become scared and paranoid enough to distort a perfectly friendly and loving conversation into something cunning and manipulative. Lord have mercy!

After a week of trying to contact my friend, we finally talked. I'd e-mailed an apology, telephoned a message of apology, and sent a gift to make up. Yet for a full week she didn't acknowledge me. That was torture because I was sorry. I really liked her and so regretted my actions.

This lady is a woman of prayer, and during this week when she wasn't talking to me, she was praying for me personally and for our relationship. After that week of silence, she called and we talked everything out. Now we're reconciled and restored. Praise the Lord!

I'm convinced that all this happened because I became so negative about simply leaving my speaking clothes behind. My negativity led me to fear, and fear led me to misunderstanding my friend. Misunderstanding led me to react negatively to her question, and my unnecessary and harsh reaction led to guilt. Guilt caused me pain and led to trying several methods to rectify the situation.

Can you imagine what might have happened if my friend was not a praying woman dedicated to following God?

Jesus warned the apostle Peter: "Simon, Simon, behold, Satan has demanded permission to sift you like wheat; but I have prayed for you, that your faith may not fail; and you, when once you have turned again, strengthen your brothers" (Luke 22:31-32 NASB). When I was thinking those negative thoughts about losing my mind, I knew better. If I'd just thought about the scripture that tells us to resist the devil and he will flee, the negative thinking and reacting would have ceased. Sometimes we're our own enemy by letting an even worse enemy run havoc in our minds.

In the book *The Three Battlegrounds*, author Frances Frangipane talks about the three battlegrounds where we fight Satan: the mind, the church, and the heavenly places. People don't have to initiate warfare; the devil has already started the war against us. Jesus warns: "Watch out that the light in you is not darkness" (Luke 11:35).

I wonder why we can't just be obedient and submit to God and resist the devil. Is that too uncomfortable for us? Are we so arrogant and full of pride that we think we can take on the devil ourselves and win?

I don't think so!

At the speaking engagement I experienced a mild case of devilment, and it broke my spirit down. I look back on that with regret.

Keeping Our Eyes on Jesus

During my ritual of dressing spiritually every morning, I call on the name of Jesus and apply His cleansing blood upon me and mine as I pray for ministering angels to protect everyone. I ask God to help me be salt and light in a world of darkness.

Wouldn't you think that would be enough to carry me to victory every day? Yes, it would—if I'd keep my mind on Jesus. But soon I turn my eyes elsewhere. I begin to succumb to mainstream thinking as I read periodicals, log on to websites, watch television, listen to the radio, or discuss current events with friends. Mercy, we're so inundated with society's mayhem, and we're often clogged up with pop culture that dictates how to conduct our lives. When we try to mix this worldly focus with godly righteousness, if we aren't careful and totally submitted to God we'll have a serious collision of the mind and spirit. We'll be dazed and wonder which direction to go.

It ain't easy resisting the devil, but it sure is possible. God said that, and that makes it true!

6

The Dynamic Duo

Good parents are responsible to teach their child, to discipline their child, to protect their child, to guide their child, and to encourage their child. Young children are so innocent that they look up to and imitate those closest to them. That's a powerful privilege and responsibility for parents.

Since my children are now grown and have their own children, I get to relax and observe them building their family relationships. The babies are clingy and dependent on their parents for everything. The younger—and older!—kids watch what their parents do, how they do it, when they do it, and who they interact with, as they gather information to function in society. The parent (or primary caregiver) is thus partnered with the child in a dynamic duo. The parent is the teacher; the child is the learner.

While I was seriously studying my Bible a few years ago, there was one doctrine that overwhelmed my heart and captivated my senses. It taught me who I am, what I am, and how I can live in a world of constant changes and challenges and come out stronger.

All my life I'd heard about the Holy Spirit being the third person in the Godhead. I heard He would convict people and guide them. I was told to never call the Holy Spirit an "it" because He's a Person. He is God, and we must give God our respect. I had sung songs such as "Spirit of the living God, fall afresh on me" and "Holy Spirit, you are welcome in this place." But did I really understand His work in my life? Not really.

My quest to find out led me to the *Open Bible* edition of the New American Standard Bible. I found what I needed. There was documented information on the teachings of the Holy Spirit (or Holy Ghost, as some refer to Him). I was excited like a little child at Christmas. Eagerly I learned about this Person who would lead me and guide me on my life journey. What joy and security and confidence we can have knowing the Holy Spirit will guide us daily and remind us of the teachings of Jesus!

We can't make it without someone greater than we are to help us along the way. The Person I want to have and must have with me 24/7 and for all the days of my life is the Holy Spirit.

Who Is the Holy Spirit?

One popular online reference source created and updated by users provides a useful starting point for our look at the Holy Spirit:

> In mainstream Christianity, the Holy Spirit or Holy Ghost is one of the three entities of the Holy Trinity which make up the single substance of God; that is, the Spirit is considered to act in concert with and share an essential nature with God the Father and God the Son (Jesus Christ)...Within Trinitarian theology, the Holy Spirit is sometimes referred to as the "Third Person" of the Triune God—with the Father being the First Person and the Son the Second Person.[1]

And here's what is taught about the Holy Spirit at an interactive Christian Bible-study website:

> The Holy Spirit was with God in the beginning and will remain with Him throughout eternity. In the Old Testament He came upon men to empower them for service for specific assignments but when they disobeyed God, the Holy Spirit left them. In the New Testament, after Pentecost, we see the Holy Spirit indwelling the believer, never to leave him, filling and empowering him for service.[2]

I'm glad to know the Holy Spirit resides in me and has been with me ever since I accepted Christ as my personal Savior when I was four years old. He has kept me from hurt, harm, and danger. He has convicted me when I'm wrong, comforted me when I was sad, covered me from punishment when I sinned, directed me when I didn't know where to go and how to go, consoled me when I was grieving, sharpened my intuition when I was wondering what was right, and given me wisdom when I was making decisions. And He's doing all those things in my life today. The Holy Spirit and I make a dynamic duo! Praise the Lord!

For the ultimate verification of who the Holy Spirit is, let's go to God's Word. The deity of the Holy Spirit is confirmed as we check out His divine attributes:

- The Spirit is everywhere present in the universe (Psalm 139:7-10).
- He has all power (Luke 1:35).
- He has all knowledge (1 Corinthians 2:10-11).
- He is eternal (Hebrews 9:14).

The Holy Spirit's deity is also revealed in that His name is linked in equality to the name of the Father and the name of the Son:

- In the baptism of the believer (Matthew 28:19).

- In the apostolic benediction (2 Corinthians 13:14).

The Spirit's deity is also seen in relation to the life and ministry of Jesus Christ:

- Jesus was conceived by the Holy Spirit (Luke 1:35).

- Jesus was anointed by the Holy Spirit for service (Acts 10:38).

- He was led by the Holy Spirit (Matthew 4:1).

- He was raised from the dead by the power of the Holy Spirit (Romans 8:11).

- Jesus gave commandments to the apostles and the church through the Holy Spirit (Acts 1:2).

Jesus depended on the Holy Spirit during His lifetime and ministry on earth. How can we do less?

Emblems of the Holy Spirit

My study of spiritual warfare led me to look at the symbols and emblems of the Holy Spirit. This prompted me to make changes in my daily communication with the Lord. Let's look closely at the Holy Spirit emblems given to us in God's Word.

The Dove

When I decided to move my business from an off-site building to my home, I turned what was then my den into an office. Separating my office area from the other living areas of my home was a wall with a cutout containing a set of shelves that bothered me. When I wasn't home much and not using this space as an office, I'd never paid attention to how cluttered the 58 x 58-inch opening looked. But now I did.

Day after day I sat there wondering what I was going to do with that opening. I asked God to give me a vision for something that would be soothing and peaceful, something that would give me the visibility to see my living room and also be a source of beauty and inspiration. My uncertainty over what to do with this space went on for weeks.

As I was sitting at my desk one day, I glanced up and suddenly saw it in my mind: a vision of a beautiful frosted-glass dove with an olive branch in its mouth. It appeared to be soaring through the air, announcing that a storm was passing and there would now be peace. I was reminded that truly the storms of life *do* pass, and we can shout hallelujah.

A glass company in Seagoville, Texas performed a masterful job in creating exactly what I wanted. Now when I sit in my office perturbed about deadlines or interruptions, I look up and am reminded that whatever trial or stress I'm in is passing by. Wonderful!

As an emblem of the Holy Spirit, the dove speaks of the Spirit's gentle, tender, peaceful nature. It signifies the peace of God that passes all understanding and is available to each of us if we allow it (Philippians 4:7). The bird symbolizes the soul of mankind, the embodiment of liberty, and the immortality of the saints—us!—through Jesus.

The Holy Spirit gives peace. This is what the Bible says about the dove:

- The dove found no resting place for the sole of her foot, and she returned into the ark to [Noah], for the waters were on the face of the whole earth. So he put out his hand and took her, and drew her into the ark to himself (Genesis 8:9).

- Though you lie down among the sheepfolds, you will be like the wings of a dove covered with silver, and her feathers with yellow gold (Psalm 68:13).

- Behold, I [Jesus] send you out as sheep in the midst of wolves. Therefore be wise as serpents and harmless as doves (Matthew 10:16).

- The Holy Spirit descended in bodily form like a dove upon [Jesus being baptized], and a voice came from heaven which said, "You are My beloved Son; in You I am well pleased" (Luke 3:22).

Fire

Nobody wants to get burned, but a lot of people are fascinated by the brilliant multicolors of fire. When I was growing up I watched my great-grandmother strike a match and burn the tip of a needle before getting a splinter out of my hand. I wondered why she was doing this, and she told me that the heat from the flame sterilized the needle to guard against infection.

The *fire* of the Holy Spirit speaks of His consuming, purifying power in the lives of believers (Acts 2:3; Isaiah 6:6-7). In my prayer and praise times, I often feel the power of God move dramatically in my life, and the fire of the Holy Spirit swells up in my body until I can sense heat in my inner being, burning on the altar of my heart. Sometimes this powerful experience causes me to weep; sometimes it causes me to tremble. Once in a while I look out into space, imagining the fire shut up in my bones—the Holy Spirit catching me on fire with His love and energy and motivation. Praise the Lord!

The Holy Spirit purifies. What does the Bible say about fire?

- For the LORD your God is a consuming fire, a jealous God (Deuteronomy 4:24).

- When the LORD has washed away the filth of the daughters of Zion, and purged the blood of Jerusalem from her midst, by the spirit of judgment and by the spirit of burning... (Isaiah 4:4).

- Who can endure the day of His coming? And who can stand when He appears? For He is like a refiner's fire and like launderer's soap. He will sit as a refiner and a purifier of silver; He will purify the sons of Levi, and purge them as gold and silver, that they may offer to the LORD an offering in righteousness (Malachi 3:2-3).

- I came to send fire on the earth, and how I wish it were already kindled! (Luke 12:49)

- There appeared to them divided tongues, as of fire, and one sat upon each of them (Acts 2:3).

- Our God is a consuming fire (Hebrews 12:29).

- Seven lamps of fire were burning before the throne, which are the seven Spirits of God (Revelation 4:5).

Wind

We can't see the wind. We know when it's blowing, and we see the results from it, but we can't bottle it, store it, capture it, or understand its hidden source. We know it's powerful.

Have you ever attempted to stand straight in a strong windstorm? Wind is powerful and as an emblem of the Holy Spirit it speaks of His mighty regenerating power that rises from hidden depths in His divinity. Listen to what Jesus said:

> The wind blows where it wishes, and you hear the sound of it, but cannot tell where it comes from and where it goes. So is everyone who is born of the Spirit (John 3:8).

The prophet Ezekiel encountered the wind of the Spirit in the Valley of Dry Bones, as God commanded:

> "Thus says the Lord GOD: 'Come from the four winds, O breath, and breathe on these slain, that they may live.'" So I prophesied as He commanded me, and breath came into them, and they lived, and stood upon their feet, an exceedingly great army (Ezekiel 37:9-10).

The wind represents the convicting power of the Holy Spirit that reveals our sins and iniquities (our dry bones) so we can turn around and be delivered. It's the wind of the Spirit that brings us to repentance and to a saving knowledge of Jesus Christ.

In Acts 2, on the day the Holy Spirit came down to earth to live in the hearts of people who believe in Jesus, "There came a sound from heaven, as of a rushing mighty wind, and it filled the whole house where they were sitting" (Acts 2:2). How wonderful and joyful that the Holy Spirit comes like the wind to provide the refreshing and invigorating breath of God in our lives.

Water

The human body needs a lot of water because water is what our bodies mostly consist of. With prolonged exercise in heat, it's possible to lose more than five liters of water, which is about ten pounds! The average, healthy human is supposed to drink as much as sixty-four ounces of water a day. Why is it so important to fill our bodies with water?

- Water sustains life. It hydrates the body so it functions properly.

- Water adjusts the body's temperature.

- Water assists in digestion.

- Water removes toxins from the body and helps create necessary body fluids.

Our bodies tell us when we need to drink more water. The physical signs of dehydration become evident, and until we get enough water, our functioning declines. Just as water is critically important to the physical body, so the "water" of the Holy Spirit is eternally significant to the spiritual body. We can't function without it.

As an emblem of the Holy Spirit, *water* speaks of His power to fill believers to overflowing with spiritual life. Here's what the Bible says:

> On the last day, that great day of the feast, Jesus stood and cried out, saying, "If anyone thirsts, let him come to Me and drink. He who believes in Me, as the Scripture has said, out of his heart will flow rivers of living water." But this He spoke concerning the Spirit, whom those believing in Him would receive; for the Holy Spirit was not yet given, because Jesus was not yet glorified (John 7:37-39).

Jesus said:

> Whoever drinks of the water that I shall give him will never thirst. But the water that I shall give him will become in him a fountain of water springing up into everlasting life (John 4:14).

Water satisfies when nothing else will. Tea, soda, lemonade, coffee, energy drinks, juices, and Kool-Aid can't take the revitalizing, energizing, body-harmonizing place of water. And nothing can substitute for the Holy Spirit. The Holy Spirit truly satisfies. Let's read more of what the Bible says about water.

- He shall come down like rain upon the grass before mowing, like showers that water the earth (Psalm 72:6).

- Therefore with joy you will draw water from the wells of salvation (Isaiah 12:3).

- Then I will sprinkle clean water on you, and you shall be clean; I will cleanse you from all your filthiness and from all your idols (Ezekiel 36:25).

- Then he brought me back to the door of the temple; and there was water, flowing from under the threshold of the temple toward the east, for the front of the temple faced east; the water was flowing from under the right side of the temple, south of the altar. He brought me out by way of the north gate, and led me around on the outside to the outer gateway that faces east; and there was water, running out on the right side.

And when the man went out to the east with the line in his hand, he measured one thousand cubits, and he brought me through the waters; the water came up to my ankles. Again he measured one thousand and brought me through the waters; the water came up to my knees. Again he measured one thousand and brought me through; the water came up to my waist. Again he measured one thousand, and it was a river that I could not cross; for the water was too deep, water in which one must swim, a river that could not be crossed. He said to me, "Son of man, have you seen this?" Then he brought me and returned me to the bank of the river.

When I returned, there, along the bank of the river, were very many trees on one side and the other. Then he said to me: "This water flows toward the eastern region, goes down into the valley, and enters the sea. When it reaches the sea, its waters are healed. And it shall be that every living thing that moves, wherever the rivers go, will live. There will be a very great multitude of fish, because these waters go there; for they will be healed, and everything will live wherever the river goes. It shall be that fishermen will stand by it from En Gedi to En Eglaim; [there] will be places for spreading their nets. Their fish will be of the same kinds as the fish of the Great Sea, exceedingly many. But its swamps and marshes will not be healed; they will be given over to salt. Along the bank of the river, on this side and that, will grow all kinds of trees used for food; their leaves will not wither, and their fruit will not fail. They will bear fruit every month, because their water flows from the sanctuary. Their fruit will be for food, and their leaves for medicine" (Ezekiel 47:1-12).

Oil

When I go into a store to get something that will soften my dry hands and feet, I look for a product that soothes, heals, and refreshes my skin. I want my skin looking bright with vitality. And when I'm spiritually dressing and anoint myself with oil that contains frankincense and myrrh, I'm reminded that I'm covered for any spiritual battles that come my way that day.

When my best friend's son was recently ordained as a pastor, I gave him a little bottle of the frankincense and myrrh oil. I told him that the oil in that bottle had no power on its own to do anything. It was simply an emblem of the Holy Spirit, and it would serve as a reminder that we daily need an anointed covering by God. We need it because every day there are battles and satanic land mines waiting to divert or destroy us.

God said, in essence, "Do not be afraid, be of good courage, and do not fear. The weapons of your warfare are not human. They are mighty to the tearing down of strongholds. They are fierce to the tearing up of the devil's kingdom. They're paramount to winning the victory over your mind and soul."

Oil represents the anointing of the Holy Spirit on the lives of all who are called to the gospel and ministry. The oil speaks of the Spirit's power to anoint us for service in God's kingdom, just as Jesus was anointed: "God anointed Jesus of Nazareth with the Holy Spirit and with power, who went about doing good and healing all who were oppressed by the devil, for God was with Him" (Acts 10:38).

The Holy Spirit anoints for service. What does the Bible say about oil and anointing?

- Oil for the light, and spices for the anointing oil and for the sweet incense (Exodus 25:6).

- You love righteousness and hate wickedness; therefore God, Your God, has anointed You with the oil of gladness more than Your companions (Psalm 45:7).

- But the wise took oil in their vessels with their lamps (Matthew 25:4).

- So [the Good Samaritan] went to him and bandaged his wounds, pouring on oil and wine; and he set him on his own animal, brought him to an inn, and took care of him (Luke 10:34).

- He who establishes us with you in Christ and has anointed us is God (2 Corinthians 1:21).

- Is anyone among you sick? Let him call for the elders of the church, and let them pray over him, anointing him with oil in the name of the Lord (James 5:14).

- You have an anointing from the Holy One, and you know all things (1 John 2:20).

Salt

Salt makes food taste more palatable, bringing out more flavor. It also preserves the freshness of food and provides essential nutrients for a healthy body. Maybe you haven't thought of salt as an emblem of the Holy Spirit, but there are many who see the Spirit's influence represented as salt in these words of Jesus:

> For everyone will be seasoned with fire, and every sacrifice will be seasoned with salt. Salt is good, but if the salt loses its flavor, how will you season it? Have salt in yourselves, and have peace with one another (Mark 9:49-50).

The Holy Spirit preserves. And the Holy Spirit within us makes us "the salt of the earth":

> You are the salt of the earth; but if the salt loses its flavor, how shall it be seasoned? It is then good for nothing but to be thrown out and trampled underfoot by men (Matthew 5:13).

The Seal

Look around your house at your household appliances, gadgets, and electronic devices. Each one of these items came with a piece of paper that signified you bought it. Along with that came an understood guarantee that the item was in good working condition, and if you found something wrong with it, you could return it for replacement or repair. Likewise, when we're grocery shopping we look for identifying marks to assure us that the food has been inspected and is safe. We often look for a respected brand-name on items we want because we believe the company's "seal" guarantees the food's quality.

At the very moment we accepted Jesus Christ as our Savior and Redeemer, we were justified, born again, and born into the body of Christ. We became temples of God. We were "sealed" or "marked" with the Holy Spirit. This seal is for security, such as when Pilate put the seal on the tomb of Jesus to make sure no one could enter without being known (Matthew 27:65-66).

Here's a thrilling thought: When we were sealed with the Holy Spirit, we were made secure in Christ. This seal of the Spirit is also a mark of ownership, like when Jeremiah bought a piece of property and the purchase deed was signed and sealed (Jeremiah 32:10). The deed meant he was now the owner. A Christian is God's property forever! The Holy Spirit is the seal of that ownership and our assurance of salvation. Here's what the Bible says about this seal of the Spirit:

- [God] also has sealed us and given us the Spirit in our hearts as a guarantee (2 Corinthians 1:22).

- Now He who has prepared us for this very thing is God, who also has given us the Spirit as a guarantee (2 Corinthians 5:5).

- In Him you also trusted, after you heard the word of truth, the gospel of your salvation; in whom also, having believed, you were sealed with the Holy Spirit of promise, who is the guarantee of our inheritance until the redemption of the purchased possession, to the praise of His glory (Ephesians 1:13-14).

The Pledge of the Holy Spirit

God sent us the Holy Spirit as a guarantee or "pledge" of what we will receive, as "a first installment" so to speak (2 Corinthians 1:22; 5:5; Ephesians 1:14). This pledge means three glorious things for us:

1. It was a down payment that sealed a bargain.

2. It represents an obligation to pay the whole price at the proper time—and thus a "guarantee." The presence of the Holy Spirit within us shows an obligation by God to redeem us completely, guaranteeing our inheritance until the future brings the total redemption of those who are God's possession.

3. It's a foretaste, a sampling, of our coming life and inheritance in God's presence.

This pledge is part of a payment agreement that secures the full sum. The Spirit's sanctification on earth is a pledge of our perfect holiness to come. The Spirit's illumination is a promise of our everlasting full light. And His comforts are the fulfilled hope of everlasting and full joy.

The Witness of the Holy Spirit

The Holy Spirit is also our witness within, assuring us of the reality of our salvation in Jesus Christ (Hebrews 10:14-18). "The Spirit Himself bears witness with our spirit that we are children of God" (Romans 8:16; see also Galatians 4:6-7). Only with the power of the Holy Spirit can we truly realize and live out the fact that God is our heavenly Father. And only with the Holy Spirit can we proclaim without reservation, "Jesus is the Lord!" (see 1 Corinthians 12:3).

The Spirit is our liberation from the power of sin and our doorway to all the privileges and blessings of Christ. So every day we should sing praises to the Holy Spirit.

You, a child of God, together with the Holy Spirit of God, create a unique and dynamic duo in the universe. Fighting together with the Spirit you can say assuredly—and even shout it from the housetop—the words our Lord spoke to His people through the prophet Isaiah:

> "No weapon formed against you shall prosper,
> And every tongue which rises against you in judgment
> You shall condemn.
> This is the heritage of the servants of the LORD,
> And their righteousness is from Me,"
> Says the LORD (Isaiah 54:17).

Are you ready to win?
Wait! There's more.

7

The Battle Is Not Ours

I've got news for you. Yes, there's good news and bad news. Let's get the negative out of the way first.

The Bad News

As we go through our day-to-day trials, it's no wonder we find it easy to believe that bumper sticker: Life is tough and then you die. Our days are saturated with heartache and trouble. We think about our problems in the morning when we arise, during the afternoon when we get a break, in the evening when things are quiet, and in the midnight hour when we should be sleeping. Sometimes we're overcome by thoughts of doom and gloom.

How many of us try to solve our own problems? We try to change other people or pray that God will do something to them if they keep messing with us. How many of us tell ourselves, "If it's not one thing, it's another"? We can't seem to get over how something we don't like is always happening to us.

Have you ever thought how you're always trying to do right while other people are doing wrong, yet they seem to get along just fine? Wouldn't it be terrific if life was fair? How wonderful it would be if all our hard work was immediately and justly rewarded. But life in this fallen world isn't like that. Instead, people will sue for something as small as a baby throwing a pebble and, they claim, it damaged their car to the tune of $600 or more. And some people lie about us or smear our reputations just because there's something about us they don't like. Some folks condemn us because we don't do or think what they want us to do or think.

Meanwhile sickness comes to the just as well as the unjust. Crime doesn't happen only in bad neighborhoods. Wars rage in places we're not even aware of. Sinister acts are committed right under our noses. Poverty is all around us. Mental illness is on the rise. Addictions are stealing the minds and strength of capable, intelligent people.

Mass media dilutes truth and imbues it with confusion. Sensationalism is the order in mainstream America. Pop culture tells us where to live; what to eat, drink, wear, and drive; what movies to watch; and what music to listen to. Foods and drinks are contaminated with unhealthy preservatives and polluted by artificial substances, putting our physical and mental well-being at risk.

The government has its own agenda, the courts have their covenants, modern medicine has its warning labels, and church has its Sunday morning theater. We're fighting abusive behavior, increasing numbers of divorces, and sexual sins of all kinds. Children bring weapons to school with the intent to kill. Suicides are on the rise. Pornography has lured many and stolen the sanctity of intimacy in marriages. Children disrespect adults, and adults aggravate children. Parents act like the children, and children are disgusted with parents. Employers mistreat employees, and employees rob their employers blind. Students are promoted via unreliable tests, while educators are forbidden to correct or fix the poor study habits and self-discipline of the students.

Cults and the occult have deadened our senses to what is right and to the true Light in the world. People are becoming more educated academically without discovering common problem-solving skills. Instead of working within the systems and guidelines of authority, people continue to defy and attempt to defraud those in charge. Changes in our economic structure have impaired our comfortable mobility to travel long distances. Hopelessness and despair, fueled by fear, are trying to overtake our lives.

But there's more news.

The Good News

As I was driving down the expressway one day three decades ago, something caught my attention. It was the illuminated bright lights on an electronic signboard. The lights were sparkling, twinkling, and scrolling. As I got closer and closer, I could read the message. The course of my life from that day to now was altered. The message? "Tough times don't last; tough people do!"

This happened on a day when my mind was centered on two schools of thought: Life will indeed be tough every day you live it and there's nothing to expect or dream because eventually you'll pass away. And when you're dead, you're done.

Oh, but friends, there's another side to this story! When I saw that message—that tough times don't last, tough people do—the condition of my mind, the transformation of my heart, and the messages in my head rotated from the bad news to the good news. As I started asking questions, my mind turned a somersault. I experienced a resurrection of confidence in the Someone who is available to me during the bad times just like He is during the good times.

You see, we can talk ourselves *into* anything and *out* of anything. The mind is the most intrinsic, overpowering force of our bodies. It's the first to be tempted by Satan and the last to be let alone by him. Thank God for giving us the ability to ask questions, analyze the possible solutions, demonstrate and evaluate our emotions in certain circumstances, and act on what we see, feel, hear, taste, and smell.

But God didn't give us the ability or the authority to fight the battles of life alone, as if He didn't exist. Satan is so crafty that we sometimes don't catch his scheme to get us to usurp God's authority in our lives. As my friend Nicole Johnson said, "We try to serve God in an advisory capacity." However, God has shown Himself fully capable of not only waging our battles for us but also *winning* every time.

Courtroom Battles

In 2005 a group I was affiliated with faced some legal challenges. I spoke to one of my good friends about what was going on. I was quite concerned about the outcome because it was a matter of survival for the group. When we learned about this challenge, some of the principals of this group fasted and prayed based on Isaiah 58. Our group had several weeks of fasting and praying together and individually. We studied the Bible and did whatever we knew to do in times of trouble.

My attitude changed when a friend told me to go to 2 Chronicles 20 and study what I found there. I remember her saying, "Why are you so stressed out about this? If you've been praying and fasting, don't you know God heard you? Are you aware that He knew this was going to happen before the foundation of the world? And, Beautiful (she calls me Beautiful!), you don't have to fight this battle. It doesn't belong to you. This battle is not yours. It belongs to the Lord." I'd known that, but it had somehow escaped me in the midst of the trial. Eugene Peterson's Bible paraphrase The Message delivers a masterful narration of this passage and the battle where God demonstrates that our battle is His:

Some time later the Moabites and Ammonites, accompanied by Meunites, joined forces to make war on Jehoshaphat. Jehoshaphat received this intelligence report: "A huge force is on its way from beyond the Dead Sea to fight you. There's no time to waste—they're already at Hazazon Tamar, the oasis of En Gedi."

Shaken, Jehoshaphat prayed. He went to GOD for help and ordered a nationwide fast. The country of Judah united in seeking GOD's help—they came from all the cities of Judah to pray to GOD.

Then Jehoshaphat took a position before the assembled people of Judah and Jerusalem at The Temple of GOD in front of the new courtyard and said, "O GOD, God of our ancestors, are you not God in heaven above and ruler of all kingdoms below? You hold all power and might in your fist—no one stands a chance against you! And didn't you make the natives of this land leave as you brought your people Israel in, turning it over permanently to your people Israel, the descendants of Abraham your friend? They have lived here and built a holy house of worship to honor you, saying, 'When the worst happens—whether war or flood or disease or famine—and we take our place before this Temple (we know you are personally present in this place!) and pray out our pain and trouble, we know that you will listen and give victory.'

"And now it's happened: men from Ammon, Moab, and Mount Seir have shown up. You didn't let Israel touch them when we got here at first—we detoured around them and didn't lay a hand on them. And now they've come to kick us out of the country you gave us. O dear God, won't you take care of them? We're helpless before this vandal horde ready to attack us. We don't know what to do; we're looking to you."

Everyone in Judah was there—little children, wives, sons—all present and attentive to GOD.

Then Jahaziel was moved by the Spirit of GOD to speak from the midst of the congregation. (Jahaziel was the son of Zechariah, the son of Benaiah, the son of Jeiel, the son of Mattaniah the Levite of the Asaph clan.) He said, "Attention everyone—all of you from out of town, all you from Jerusalem, and you King Jehoshaphat—GOD's word: Don't be afraid; don't pay any mind to this vandal horde. This is God's war, not yours. Tomorrow you'll go after them; see, they're already on their way up the slopes of Ziz; you'll meet them at the end of the ravine near the wilderness of Jeruel. You won't have to lift a hand in this battle; just stand firm, Judah and Jerusalem, and watch GOD's saving work for you take shape. Don't be afraid, don't waver. March out boldly tomorrow—GOD is with you."

Then Jehoshaphat knelt down, bowing with his face to the ground. All Judah and Jerusalem did the same, worshiping GOD. The Levites (both Kohathites and Korahites) stood to their feet to praise GOD, the God of Israel; they praised at the top of their lungs!

They were up early in the morning, ready to march into the wilderness of Tekoa. As they were leaving, Jehoshaphat stood up and said, "Listen Judah and Jerusalem! Listen to what I have to say! Believe firmly in GOD, your God, and your lives will be firm! Believe in your prophets and you'll come out on top!"

After talking it over with the people, Jehoshaphat appointed a choir for GOD; dressed in holy robes, they were to march ahead of the troops, singing,

> Give thanks to GOD,
> His love never quits.

As soon as they started shouting and praising, GOD set ambushes against the men of Ammon, Moab, and Mount Seir as they were attacking Judah, and they all ended up dead. The Ammonites and Moabites mistakenly attacked those from Mount Seir and massacred them. Then, further confused, they went at each other, and all ended up killed.

As Judah came up over the rise, looking into the wilderness for the horde of barbarians, they looked on a killing field of dead bodies—not a living soul among them...

Jehoshaphat then led all the men of Judah and Jerusalem back to Jerusalem—an exuberant parade. GOD had given them joyful relief from their enemies! They entered Jerusalem and came to The Temple of GOD with all the instruments of the band playing.

When the surrounding kingdoms got word that GOD had fought Israel's enemies, the fear of God descended on them. Jehoshaphat heard no more from them; as long as Jehoshaphat reigned, peace reigned (2 Chronicles 20:1-24,27-30).

This ancient account of God fighting and winning the battle gave me hope. Now let me share a new-covenant, modern, baby-boomer version. The group I was involved in was sued by an enemy alleging facts that simply weren't true. So we prayed that God would remove this false indictment, and that nothing would come of it. But God didn't move the way we'd hoped. It went to trial four years after the initial indictment.

During the days of waiting for the trial, we used due diligence in securing an attorney as well as making sure all the documentation was in order, even having audits of policies and procedures done. The group knew nothing brought up against them could stand because right was done and was attested to in the documentation. The representing attorney charged only for out-of-pocket and court costs because the group was in such a great position because of their integrity.

Unfortunately, it turned out the attorney for the group wasn't the best in documentation, investigation, and court room presentation. The plaintiff's lawyer was eloquent, forceful, and convincing. We lost the case big time. Needless to say, we were devastated.

God's Hand in the Battle

When I was told what happened and how angry and disappointed the other members were, I suggested we go into prayer and fasting, according to Isaiah 58, and that our prayers should be for God to direct our paths. An injustice was done, and we didn't know what to do next. Most of the group complied with this suggestion, and a series of prayer meetings and fasting took place. A leader in the group received a telephone call about an appeals attorney who was interested in the case. This was an open door.

Several people met with that attorney and agreed to pay him on an installment basis for his help. The attorney drastically reduced his fees to help out. Researching the case, the new attorney found major discrepancies and knew this case needed to be tried again with all the facts presented and the pitfalls of the previous case exposed. The judge agreed, and the case went back to trial.

At that point I asked each member of the group to study 2 Chronicles 20. When we got together and discussed the Jehoshaphat incident, we found four critical points:

1. Jehoshaphat was a leader who trusted God.

2. Jehoshaphat was humble enough to pray to God in front of the people.

3. Jehoshaphat was in-tune enough to listen to the voice of God.

4. Jehoshaphat was obedient enough to follow God's instructions.

You read the result of Jehoshaphat's obedience. He called forth the singers and appointed a choir dressed in holy robes to march ahead of the troops singing, "Give thanks to GOD, His love never quits." The enemies who came to destroy Jehoshaphat and his hosts got confused and killed each other.

We ought to be up on our feet shouting and dancing at the work of God's hands in this major battle! I'm now sitting in my chair but my body is shaking as I think about the awesome power of God to destroy our enemies. We don't have to lift a finger! What we *must* do is *be obedient*.

After we studied this story, I advised the group members to stop praying and fasting. I said to stop worrying and losing sleep. If God moved for Jehoshaphat in the Old Testament when Jesus was concealed, how much more will He move for us—New Testament people who are in the dispensation of grace under the blood covering of Jesus Christ?

We were in the best position because we had our heavenly advocate, Jesus, sitting at the right hand of Father God and pleading our case for us. And we had an earthly advocate, the Holy Spirit, living inside us to guide us into righteousness. We had everything taken care of—the trusting in God, the praying to God, and the listening to God's voice. What we had to choose to do now was be obedient to God. Just as He told Jehoshaphat to sing before Him and do nothing further until He told them to, that was what our group had to do. Our instructions were to thank God for the victory (though we couldn't see it yet) and sing praises to Him aloud (and in our minds when singing aloud was not appropriate).

When the people in our group went into the court room to testify, they were to have a song in their hearts. The song was Psalm 106:1: "Oh, give thanks to the LORD, for He is good! For His mercy endures forever."

A New Verdict

Are you ready for the result? Have you guessed already? The testimony went well the first day, with the appellate attorney uncovering important facts that were omitted in the first trial. Everybody on our group's side testified effectively. At the end of the second day I received a call that went something like this: "Mrs. Wells, I can't believe what happened today. When the judge asked a question of the plaintiff's attorney, the attorney forgot what the case was about.

He was so confused the judge got annoyed and called for the case to resume tomorrow. He told the confused attorney to have his cases straight when he gets back in the morning."

I was a bit surprised, but I recalled what we had done and what Jehoshaphat and his people had done. I thanked God on the spot.

The third day of the trial was even more dramatic. The plaintiff's attorneys came with overhead transparencies for exhibits. When it was time to show them, they were so confused they couldn't find them. Even after a recess they were scrambling to find what they'd planned to present. The judge was irritated again and ended the testimony. The jury was sent to the jury room to deliberate.

While the jury was out, the plaintiff told her attorneys to drop the charges. But before they could, the jury came back and delivered a verdict of not guilty. The judge ruled the case was sealed and could never be reopened.

We got far more than we prayed for. We had prayed and fasted and begged God to either let the plaintiff drop the charges or for the jury to find us not guilty. God granted *both* of these—and more— because the judge sealed the case forever.

This war was not fought by us. The battle was the Lord's. Can you imagine how terrible it would have been if we'd taken this matter into our own hands without trusting the Lord? Can you imagine how we could have messed up our reputation, our finances, and our stability if we chose to march to our own drumbeat or to any drummer but the Lord?

I can't guarantee any legal circumstance you might face will turn out this way or that situations will work out the way you desire. But I can say with certainty that when you let the God of the universe, who knows all about your situation, guide you into what to do, you're then in the center of His will. And His perfect will operates in the supernatural to your ultimate advantage in the natural. Let Jesus fix the situation for you.

Sing this Negro spiritual with me:

All I want, all I want,
all I want is a little more faith in Jesus.
Whenever we meet you here we say,
A little more faith in Jesus.

Since that time I've been thinking and praying about the phenomenon of this miracle of God to deliver the group I was part of from the verdict rendered in the first trial. Yes, obedience was key. But I believe that equally important was the fact that we praised God and gave Him glory in the middle of the battle. When we started singing praise to God and honoring Him for His goodness, we didn't have a clue of what was going to happen in our valley of trouble. We were singing and shouting and blessing God during the most critical part of the battle. When we were defeated, we still told God how wonderful He was and thanked Him for His lovingkindness and tender mercy.

When the children of God honor Him with their praise, worship Him in their hearts, and caress Him in their minds, there's nothing good that God will withhold from them. During the obedience of praise and worship God brought my group out of danger and into the marvelous position of rescue.

Can You Do It?

Can *you* be obedient? Can you praise the Lord in the middle of adversity? Can you trust God enough to know He'll protect you and fight for you even when it doesn't look like the situation is going to work out for you? Will you continue to trust Him when circumstances all around seem discouraging and look like a disaster? Are you willing to seek the Lord for instructions and follow the Holy Spirit's directions regardless of what other people say or think?

Is this easy—this believing, listening, and waiting on God? *No!* This is one of the hardest commitments in life. Thinking that turning to and following Jesus should be easy is what keeps some people from reaching the goals God has for them and from winning the battle the enemy brings to them. God has given us the capacity to think and to make choices without always having to ask Him what He thinks. No-brainer decisions come about when our relationship with God is so vital that we walk with Him and talk to Him all day. We pray without ceasing. When we wake up in the morning our minds are on Jesus. We walk through the day thinking about how good Jesus is. We tell everyone we can about the love of Jesus we experience every day. Our stronghold is Jesus. This is the scenario when we can just make a decision and it will be done because we're in the perfect will of God and we think God-thoughts because we're dedicated to Him. His will for our lives will come to pass. Unfortunately this is humanly impossible to attain 24/7. But we have God and His tremendous love, mercy, and grace on our side!

The Will of God

> The will of God will never take you
> Where the grace of God cannot keep you,
> Where the arms of God cannot support you,
> Where the riches of God cannot supply your needs,
> Where the power of God cannot endow you.
>
> The will of God will never take you
> Where the Spirit of God cannot work through you,
> Where the wisdom of God cannot teach you,
> Where the army of God cannot protect you,
> Where the hands of God cannot mold you.
>
> The will of God will never take you,
> Where the love of God cannot enfold you,
> Where the mercies of God cannot sustain you,
> Where the peace of God cannot calm your fears,
> Where the authority of God cannot overrule for you.
>
> The will of God will never take you
> Where the comfort of God cannot dry your tears,

Where the Word of God cannot feed you,
Where the miracles of God cannot be done for you,
Where the omnipresence of God cannot find you.

Everything happens for a purpose.
We may not see the wisdom of it all now,
but trust and believe in the Lord
that everything is for the best.

AUTHOR UNKNOWN

God is still in the miracle-working business. If you don't believe this, talk to Him and read His Word. Don't take my word for it. I know He is because He's come through for me with techniques and tactics that I didn't understand and, frankly, ones that at times I didn't like.

A Simple Answer

I mentioned that once when I had a dispute with a business firm I went away for a week to fast and pray for God to give me a strategy for dealing with the injustices of a business deal.

I just knew that during this time God would give me the ABCs to handle this. I kept my pencil and paper ready to record everything God said. Since seven is said to be the number of completion, I figured that on the seventh day He would speak so I would know exactly what to do. I was so confident.

Well, I started hearing from God on the first day, but I knew He had more to say. The second, third, fourth, fifth, and sixth days He said the same thing. I didn't hear Him speak audibly, but I knew He was speaking in my spirit. I got all primed and ready for the seventh-day revelation. On that day I was very still and quiet. I turned off all the music and any sounds that might hinder my hearing from Him. I intensely sought the voice of almighty God.

For a whole twenty-four hours I listened. I kept hearing the same sound bite from God I'd heard the other six days, but I was sure there was more…but there wasn't. God had been speaking to me all the time but not according to what I wanted. I was looking for a natural, human strategy. He gave me a supernatural strategy I didn't want to recognize. What He said was, "Trust Me." That's it. *"Trust Me!"*

I finally got it. It took me an entire week of listening—a week of intensity, nervousness, and bondage to my expectations—to hear the simple-but-powerful voice of God saying simply, "Trust Me."

Oh, what a relief! I finally realized I didn't have to do any negotiations, engage in arguments, deal with anger, try to persuade, or fight. God would work it out.

When I got back to my office, I was determined to wait on God. The deadline set by the business meant nothing anymore. My desire meant nothing to me. I was set in my heart to do only what God told me. I was going to trust Him.

For eight months I did nothing. The company had claimed they needed an answer from me within ten days, but I did absolutely nothing but thank God for relieving me of dealing with the situation. Every time I thought about it, I said, "Thank You, Jesus!" and went on with the business of the moment.

In the eighth month of waiting on the Lord for resolution, I heard His voice in my spirit say, "Call now." I picked up the telephone and called my contact at the business. After greeting him, I said, "I need you to sign the contract I submitted earlier to your company and return it to me by three o'clock tomorrow afternoon. Thank you." The very brief conversation was over. The situation ended the following afternoon when I received via Federal Express the signed contract.

That business battle wasn't mine; it was the Lord's. When I allowed Him to move, He worked it out according to His will. God's deadlines are not our deadlines, and His ways are not our ways (Isaiah 55:8). We must trust in the Lord. We need to humble ourselves under His mighty hand. So listen to the still small voice of

God and be obedient. Praise Him and be grateful, for He is God. His mercy is everlasting.

Think of some times you've believed, trusted, listened to, and obeyed God. Note them and list the results. Remember how God fought and won the battle for you. Praise Him!

- _____

- _____

- _____

- _____

- _____

8

Weapons for Winning

Remember how I get spiritually "dressed" in the morning?

- *I fix my hair.* I put on the helmet of salvation.
- *I pad my bra.* I put on the breastplate of righteousness.
- *I tighten my girdle.* I put on the girdle (or belt) of truth.
- *I put on my stomping shoes.* I put on belief and praise.
- *I grab my shield and sword.* I declare my faith and trust in God and His Word.

This is my reminder to put on the armor of God:

Be strong in the Lord and in his mighty power. Put on the full armor of God so that you can take your stand against the devil's schemes. For our struggle is not against flesh and blood, but against the rulers, against the authorities, against the powers of this dark world and against the spiritual forces of evil in the heavenly realms. Therefore put on the full armor of God, so that when the day of evil comes, you may be able to stand your ground, and after you have done everything, to stand. Stand firm then, with the belt of truth buckled around your waist, with the breastplate of righteousness in place, and with your feet fitted with the readiness that comes from the gospel of peace. In addition to all this, take up the shield of faith, with which you can extinguish all the flaming arrows of the evil one. Take the helmet of salvation and the sword of the Spirit, which is the word of God. And pray in the Spirit on all occasions with all kinds of prayers and requests. With this in mind, be alert and always keep on praying for all the saints (Ephesians 6:10-18 NIV).

The Fight Is On!

When I was a little girl kids who wanted to fight at school said, "Put up your dukes!" That meant to raise your arms, ball up your fists, and get ready to hit. Those were scary words if you thought you'd lose, and they were motivating words if you thought you had the upper hand. To onlookers that phrase meant there was going to be free and interesting entertainment.

The fighting kids usually got into trouble because the school didn't tolerate that kind of behavior. In fact, as I shared in chapter 1, I fought Heddie Ruth. And sure enough, I got into trouble. The previous two days when she'd attacked me, her actions somehow escaped official notice. But after I fought back on the third afternoon, Mrs. Jackson called me into her room the following day and reprimanded me. She reminded me that I'd never been in trouble and that I was considered one of the nicest and smartest girls at school. She was surprised that I had "lowered" myself to engage in a fistfight. She'd thought of me as an example of fine young womanhood. She let me know I should never fight or handle myself in such a barbaric way again. She pointed out that I was too intelligent and too well respected to allow somebody to pull me down to his or her level. I was supposed to work to bring people up to my level.

The part that really got me thinking was when she told me that a good reputation was critical to becoming successful. If I marred my reputation, the bad would follow me and limit me for the rest of my life. But if I had a good reputation, it would follow me and open doors. So I needed to watch what I did and watch how I presented myself—being careful about what I said, how I said it, and about the people I socialized with. Anybody who made me less than my best wasn't a good person to associate with.

A Better Way?

As I left Mrs. Jackson's room, I realized that there are some times when a person has to fight physically but usually there's a better way. Since that day, in every situation where I'm challenged to fight, I remember Mrs. Jackson's words and try my best to live up to them. The same strategy for winning the battles of life hinges on those words of reproof from my caring teacher. Our reputations *do* follow us for the rest of our lives, so we must be careful how we act and talk. We're fighting for our lives every day. Thankfully we have a Teacher who has given us the strategies to fight skillfully and win overwhelmingly. Jesus has armored us as soldiers going into combat. Like it or not, we are *soldiers* for Christ.

In the armed forces of the world, soldiers come in all shapes, sizes, nationalities, colors, denominations, backgrounds, mental states, levels of physical dexterity, and socioeconomic standings. But there are many things they have in common. The most important is they are always ready for battle. We need to be that way too. We must keep our weapons and ammunition with us and ready to use every minute of the day. We must be ready to submit ourselves to the mighty hand of God and say no to the devil, to worldly systems, to the flesh, and to the opinions of family and friends if necessary.

Submission, even to God, isn't easy for control freaks like me. To concede that I wasn't in control was one of the hardest facts I had to face—and I still struggle with it.

In 1994, however, I totally submitted everything to the Lord. And I mean *everything*—my career, life, family, money, church, thoughts, ideas, dreams, body, soul, and spirit. Although I became a Christian at the age of four and understood what I was doing, it took me several decades to realize all my commitment meant and required. When I humbled myself under the mighty hand of God and asked Jesus into my heart, I entered a fight against the devil. But I didn't know it. I struggled with feelings and situations of turmoil, as most people do, but I fought back using my own physical and emotional resources, often wearing the heavy and ineffective armor of humanity instead of the armor God provides. Therefore I suffered countless wounds and defeats because I had chosen the wrong weapons.

Now I Know How to Fight

But thanks to God, I now know how to wage and win the war against Satan. I follow the commandments found in the Word of God without fear of defeat and ask Jesus for help and strength. I hold my head high when I'm being mistreated and smile as I watch God defend me. I walk into opposition with calmness and clarity, knowing the Holy Spirit will guide me. I sense the unction of the Holy Spirit telling me when, and what to do when, in my humanness, I'm not sure how to respond. I breathe easy when I come into contact with danger and feel God's ministering angels taking charge to sustain me in Christ. I can launch into deep, uncharted waters holding onto faith. God keeps His promises whether I can see them now or they come about in the future.

I can do all this because the fight is on—and I know what to do:

- *Pray.* I wake up in the morning with my mind on Jesus. And I'm praying to my heavenly Father. Prayer opens the communication link between God and me.

- *Praise and worship.* I saturate my home and car with praise music. I humble myself and worship God in my private sanctuary. Praise and worship encourage me and honors God as I share my love and respect for Him.

- *The Word.* Bible reading is exciting, uplifting, and challenging as I explore the concepts, precepts, and teachings. Studying the Bible enhances my ability to hear what God is telling me. As I meditate on His words day and night, I'm encouraged by the ways He acts on my behalf even when I don't know it.

- *Seek God's advice.* I seek answers and understanding from God and from wise believers He brings into my life. I trust these believers to pray before they offer counsel. I have a spiritual accountability person, Debra, who has never steered me in a wrong direction. I consult my husband, who thinks through situations and asks God for wisdom before telling me his insights. My children are also a vital part of my godly advice cadre. Because they're Christians and because they practice their faith in God, we can work things out together for the good of the situation and the glory of God. Sometimes we've misunderstood God's directions, but His grace and mercy are boundless and everlasting!

Armor is for soldiers and for fighting. We are soldiers in God's army, and He gives us protection!

God's "Dress for Success" Regimen

"Take up the whole armor of God, that you may be able to withstand in the evil day, and having done all, to stand" (Ephesians 6:13).

Helmet of Salvation

Breastplate of Righteousness

Shield of Faith

Belt of Truth

Sword of the Spirit (The Word of God)

Gospel of Peace (Shoes)

Figure 1: The Armor of God

Everybody who has met me knows I love to be flashy. Bling-bling is my thing. My clothes always have some kind of decoration on them somewhere, and I always wear a bee pin. The bee is my logo, and my motto is, "In Christ, you can *bee* the best!" If the bumblebee can defy the odds of aerodynamics and fly when it's not capable of flying (according to the laws of science), then human beings can defy the odds of the devil when we're not capable of it (according to society). The Master Scientist and the Creator of society says, "You *can* because I am the I AM":

- *I Am* above every mountain you have to climb.
- *I Am* under every valley you go through.
- *I Am* centered in every storm that rages in your life.
- *I Am* in every river you must cross.
- *I Am* over every height that blocks your way.
- *I Am* in every whirlwind that spins you around.
- *I Am* weeping with you in your tear-filled bed.
- *I Am* standing with you in every courtroom.
- *I Am* sitting with you in every hospital room.
- *I Am* listening every time you call.
- *I Am* walking with you through grief and pain.
- *I Am* studying with you for and in every academic test.
- *I Am* grieving with you when you're abused.
- *I Am* holding you when you're depressed.
- *I Am* your anchor when a spouse or friend walks out on you.
- *I Am* the redeemer of your children when they go astray.
- *I Am* protecting you when you're frightened.

- *I Am* comforting you when you're lonely.

- *I Am* sustaining you when your business is about to fold.

- *I Am* creating wealth for you when you're in poverty.

- *I Am* your heart's desire when you have no hope.

- *I Am* your way-maker when there seems to be no path.

- *I Am* your trusted friend when you have no friends.

- *I Am* your wisdom when you make foolish mistakes.

- *I Am* your forgiver when you sin against me, yourself, or others.

- *I Am* your safety in times of danger.

- *I Am* your confidence when you feel incompetent.

- *I Am* your justice when fairness fails.

- *I Am* your light in darkness when you can't find your way.

- *I Am* your stabilizer when your emotions run rampant.

- *I Am* your teacher when you have lessons to learn.

- *I Am* your chastiser when you need a reprimand.

- *I Am* your mercy-giver when you need mercy.

- *I Am* your grace-giver when you need grace.

- *I Am* your reminder when you forget about Me.

- *I Am* your refuge when you need a hiding place.

- *I Am* your strength when you're falling apart.

- *I Am* your healer when your body or heart is sick.

- *I Am* your source when your resources are gone.

- *I Am* your pardon when you're guilty.

- *I Am* your patience when you're too hasty.

- *I Am* your kindness when you're grumpy.

- *I Am* your buffer when you need someone to intercede.

- *I Am* your intelligent interpreter when you don't understand.

- *I Am* your joy in times of sorrow.

- *I Am* your peace-speaker when you're anxious.

- *I Am* your solid rock when your feet are slipping.

- *I Am* your ability to stand tall when people speak evil against you.

- *I Am* your mind-regulator when you don't know who you are or what your life purpose is.

- *I Am* your mother, father, sister, and brother when you're all alone.

- I *Am* your Adonai, your Lord, your Master.

- I *Am* your El Shaddai, your almighty God.

- I *Am* your battle axe.

- I *Am* your victory in times of war.

Who Is God to You?

Who is the great *I Am* to you? Write it down and include your insights.

- _____

_____

_____

- _____

_____

_____

- _____

_____

_____

- _____

_____

_____

- _____

_____

_____

I'm so glad we don't have to wear real metal armor and carry massive weapons to fight Satan and his minions. We just have to don God's armor. So put on your fighting clothes! And people don't have to know what we have on. We just have to know ourselves what we're wearing and why. We want to be prepared for each battle.

9

Fixing Our Hair

Take the helmet of salvation...
EPHESIANS 6:17

I was at Salon Charis, my daughter Lesa's beauty salon in DeSoto, Texas, and I asked the hair stylists: "In your training to be professional hair stylists and consultants, what did you learn about the necessity of the hair on our heads?"

They looked at me and each other and then told me they didn't learn anything about the necessity of hair.

That was a bit strange because I'd assumed that the use and necessity of hair would have been included in their training, kind of like how musicians study music theory. Our conversation continued as they gave their opinions about the use and necessity of hair. Their comments included hair being a covering for the head and protection from heat or cold. Plus hair gives us opportunities to change how we look depending on how we're feeling at the moment. We also feel good when we have our hair clean and fixed up.

Somebody mentioned how hair is our natural covering God gave to insulate our brains. Our brain coordinates body functions and movements. If it is damaged or malfunctions, everything else does too, sometimes causing catastrophic results. If the brain is hurt the whole body suffers. If the mind is messed up, our entire beings are messed up. And our brains are our thinking center. How we think often defeats us. Our thinking is revealed by how we talk and what we do. What are you thinking right now? Are you wondering, *What's hair got to do with life anyway?*

Think about it. Hair performs various functions for humans and animals:

- Hair forms an insulating coat. It traps a layer of air just outside the skin, thereby reducing loss of heat.
- Hair absorbs harmful radiation from the sun.
- Hair keeps coarse dust particles away from the scalp.
- Other body hair lessens the friction between limbs and body.
- Hair beautifies the body and imparts color.
- Hair protects from rain.
- Hair lets us express our personalities and attitudes.
- When animals are in danger their hair stands on end and provides protection by making them look bigger.
- Hair can help blend animals in with their surroundings, helping them escape watchful eyes of enemies.

Okay, maybe so much emphasis on hair is a bit over the top. After all, people who are bald seem to do just fine. So let's look at our heads of hair as a symbol of what's inside our heads—our thinking. Have you had a bad hair day lately? In my life, I've battled wrong thinking a lot. But if I can go to the beauty shop and get my hair together or use a curling iron to make myself look good, I certainly should be able to use the tools God provides to get my mind fixed when I'm having a bad-mind day. I can't find out how to fix my mind in a hairstyling book, but I do have a book I can reference that will change my style of thinking and regroup my mental functions so I can better fight off the wiles of the devil.

Battling Idle Thoughts

What are you thinking right this minute? Does it glorify God? My great-grandmother often said, "An idle mind is the devil's workshop." Idle thoughts are often *idol* centered. They're usually thoughts of foolishness, devilment, hatred, malice, tricks, schemes, gossip, lies, perversion, control, over-indulging, destruction, delay, or mindless drivel. Have you had thoughts like these?

If you answer yes, you have a lot of company—the rest of humanity! But there's great news for us! God gives us clarity on what to do. He tells us:

> Let this mind be in you which was also in Christ Jesus, who, being in the form of God, did not consider it robbery to be equal with God, but made Himself of no reputation, taking the form of a bondservant, and coming in the likeness of men (Philippians 2:5-7).

The apostle Paul tells us that we're to think like Jesus because as He is, so we ought to be in the world. That's also what the apostle John points us to: "As He is, so are we in this world" (1 John 4:17). How does Jesus think? What does He have on His mind? Love and happiness, truth and justice, and most of all the glory and praise of God.

Throughout the Scriptures—from Genesis through Revelation—God the Father and Jesus the Son talk to us about living life. Dwell on these wonderful love scriptures for a while.

- For God so *loved* the world that He gave His only begotten Son, that whoever believes in Him should not perish but have everlasting life (John 3:16).

- A new commandment I give to you, that you *love* one another; as I have *loved* you, that you also *love* one another (John 13:34).

- He who has My commandments and keeps them, it is he who *loves* Me. And he who *loves* Me will be *loved* by My Father, and I will *love* him and manifest Myself to him (John 14:21).

- If anyone *loves* Me, he will keep My word; and My Father will *love* him, and We will come to him and make Our home with him (John 14:23).

- Greater *love* has no one than this, than to lay down one's life for his friends. You are My friends if you do whatever I command you (John 15:13-14).

- Who shall separate us from the *love* of Christ? Shall tribulation, or distress, or persecution, or famine, or nakedness, or peril, or sword?... In all these things we are more than conquerors through Him who *loved* us. For I am persuaded that neither death nor life, nor angels nor principalities nor powers, nor things present nor things to come, nor height nor depth, nor any other created thing, shall be able to separate us from the *love* of God which is in Christ Jesus our Lord (Romans 8:35-39).

- Walk in *love*, as Christ also has *loved* us and given Himself for us, an offering and a sacrifice to God for a sweet-smelling aroma (Ephesians 5:2).

- Husbands, *love* your wives, just as Christ also *loved* the church and gave Himself for her (Ephesians 5:25).

- He who does not *love* does not know God, for God is *love* (1 John 4:8).

- And we have known and believed the *love* that God has for us. God is *love*, and he who abides in *love* abides in God, and God in him (1 John 4:16).

- We *love* Him because He first *loved* us (1 John 4:19).

- Keep yourselves in the *love* of God, looking for the mercy of our Lord Jesus Christ unto eternal life (Jude 21).

Blessed Also Means Happy

Think about this happiness message (the Beatitudes) from the Sermon on the Mount in chapter 5 of the book of Matthew:

And seeing the multitudes, He went up on a mountain, and when He was seated His disciples came to Him. Then He opened His mouth and taught them, saying:

"Blessed are the poor in spirit,
  for theirs is the kingdom of heaven.
Blessed are those who mourn,
  for they shall be comforted.
Blessed are the meek,
  for they shall inherit the earth.
Blessed are those who hunger and thirst for righteousness,
  for they shall be filled.
Blessed are the merciful,
  for they shall obtain mercy.
Blessed are the pure in heart,
  for they shall see God.
Blessed are the peacemakers,
  for they shall be called sons of God.
Blessed are those who are persecuted for righteousness'
  sake, for theirs is the kingdom of heaven.
Blessed are you when they revile and persecute you, and
  say all kinds of evil against you falsely for My sake.
  Rejoice and be exceedingly glad, for great is your reward
  in heaven, for so they persecuted the prophets who
  were before you" (Matthew 5:1-12).

Jesus thought pure thoughts. He knew He was righteous and our Messiah. He knew nothing was impossible with God when we pray and let Him have His way. Jesus lived an obedient life, clearly proclaiming God's authority and the authority He had as the Son of God. His thoughts were the thoughts of His Father. His mind was the mind of God.

What a profound lesson in Christlike thinking we find in Paul's words to the Philippian believers:

> [Jesus] made Himself of no reputation, taking the form of a bondservant, and coming in the likeness of men. And being found in appearance as a man, He humbled Himself and became obedient to the point of death, even the death of the cross. Therefore God also has highly exalted Him and given Him the name which is above every name, that at the name of Jesus every knee should bow, of those in heaven, and of those on earth, and of those under the earth, and that every tongue should confess that Jesus Christ is Lord, to the glory of God the Father (Philippians 2:7-11).

We can change our stinking thinking to godly thinking if we're willing to lay down our own agendas and thoughts and keep our minds focused on Jesus.

When you "fix your hair" (your mind) in this way, you're styling yourself to make God look good through you. You're protecting your mind from the idleness of this present age. Through the mouths of people whose heads are covered by the helmet of salvation comes mighty prayers. We're told to always pray and not faint or be weary. To keep our minds on Jesus, we're to pray to the Father in His Son's name, remembering that the prayers of the righteous avail much. Doesn't this great news make you want to sing?

> Turn your eyes upon Jesus,
> Look full in His wonderful face,
> And the things of earth will grow strangely dim,
> In the light of His glory and grace.[1]

If we'll just remember to keep our minds and eyes upon Jesus, the Author and Finisher of our faith, our thoughts will be clean, and we won't fall to idleness. Let's do what God's Word says: "Let us who are of the day be sober, putting on the breastplate of faith and love, and as a helmet the hope of salvation" (1 Thessalonians 5:8).

God Has a Plan

So "fix your hair" by putting on the helmet of salvation that guards your mind (your thought life). Remember, the battle is against the enemy who attacks us via our thinking. By following, heeding, loving, and serving Jesus, we are assured of life eternal with Him.

God has a plan and a purpose for your life, which includes being victorious. Keep your mind stayed on Jesus. Just think of His goodness to you. As the old adage says, "A mind is a terrible thing to waste."

Holy Father, please show me the areas in my thought life that need to come under subjection to You. I want to have a clean heart and clean mind to walk victoriously before You. I want to win!

10

Padding Our Bras

With the breastplate of righteousness in place…
EPHESIANS 6:14 NIV

What's a Bra Got to Do with It?

After contemplating the role of hair in our lives, my thoughts turned to bras. Odd, I know, but, well, that's what happened. In talking with the stylists at my daughter's salon, bras came up and they chimed in with their take. Through serious insights and occasional laughter we documented the uses of bras.

Bras are support garments. They bind us. They strengthen our upper bodies. They hold us in place. They brace our backs and upper torsos. They enhance stability. They give us confidence. They improve our appearance.

Did you know bras are for men too? They're used in athletic activities to secure posture, strengthen the upper body, and shield perspiration. They're also used by military and law enforcement personnel, in the form of bullet-proof vests for example, but also to help protect the body from extreme wet, cold, or heat. In each case the main purposes are to shield and protect.

Safeguarding Our Hearts

A protective vest or body-shield safeguards the body against injury that could come through dangerous weapons, electrical shocks, severe weather, sports, exercise, and accidents. If law enforcement officers and soldiers aren't wearing such protection, they may get seriously injured in their line of work. That's also why in many hazardous jobs workers are required to wear some kind of protection over their upper body.

Spiritually speaking, as we're putting on the armor of God, it would be foolish to leave off the breastplate, which works in conjunction with the shield of faith. They both protect against being wounded or struck down. The breastplate is worn on the chest, and in biblical times it was the most important piece of armor soldiers wore. It protected their hearts and other vital organs. Because the heart circulates life-blood through the body, if it's even slightly injured, the body doesn't function at it best. If the blood that flows through the heart is contaminated, the entire body is harmed. Compromised blood causes sickness, disease, heart attacks, and impaired motor skills and mental ability.

Nothing works right when blood isn't flowing properly. Clots may form that may lead to fatal blockage in the arteries. The contamination of the heart is like the filth in a vacuum cleaner that hasn't been emptied for a long time. The more you vacuum, the more dirt falls back on the floor.

How's Your Heart?

What's flowing in your heart? Does it please God? What a person thinks in his heart, that's the way he really is (see Proverbs 23:7).

I've heard people say (and I've been guilty of it myself) that they couldn't forgive someone for hurting them. Have you ever wanted to pay someone back for something bad that happened to you or someone you love? Or, do you envy what people have?

Maybe you wish something bad would happen to someone so you can point a finger at him or her? Have you been indiscreet with someone? Have you cheated when filling out forms or documents? Have you deliberately created confusion or strife at church or in another organization? Are you jealous of your spouse or another family member? Have you ignored someone because you didn't think she met your standards? Are you prejudiced against a person's ethnicity, denomination, living conditions, or educational status? Do you have a greedy or ungrateful heart? Do you hold grudges or think about doing wrong things?

When you have anger, bitterness, vengeance, violence, and vindictiveness on your mind you're spreading filth back into your heart. If any of these heart and mind ailments of demonic manifestations are part of your frequent activities, the dirt is overflowing. Empty the bag and ask God to cleanse your heart from all unrighteousness.

The Best Righteousness

In the Old Testament a righteous person is upright, just, straight, innocent, true, and sincere. This standing is the product of a person's moral actions in accordance with the divine plan under the law of God.

In the New Testament we receive the great news that our standing of righteousness comes with salvation through the righteousness of Jesus Christ. There's absolutely nothing we can humanly do physically and emotionally to make ourselves righteous. There is none righteous but the Father. And He declares that our self-proclaimed righteousness is a filthy rag in His sight (Isaiah 64:6). Righteousness, like the kingdom of heaven, is God's gift to us through His grace (Matthew 5:6; 6:33).

The apostle James said faith without works is dead and righteous acts include works of charity as well as avoiding sins.

How can true righteousness be ours? The Message paraphrase of Romans 3:21-24 helps make it plain:

> But in our time something new has been added. What Moses and the prophets witnessed to all those years has happened. The God-setting-things-right that we read about has become Jesus-setting-things-right for us. And not only for us, but for everyone who believes in him. For there is no difference between us and them in this.
>
> Since we've compiled this long and sorry record as sinners (both us and them) and proved that we are utterly incapable of living the glorious lives God wills for us, God did it for us. Out of sheer generosity he put us in right standing with himself. A pure gift. He got us out of the mess we're in and restored us to where he always wanted us to be. And he did it by means of Jesus Christ.

When we accept Jesus as our personal Lord and Savior, we're instantly placed in a right (righteous) standing before God. Our hearts get a holy transplant and our minds undergo holy brain surgery; we become righteous new creations in Christ Jesus. So why do we still have malice in our hearts? Check your salvation. Check your prayer life and your Bible-study time and your intimate time with Jesus. Are you spending enough time with the Lord for Him to communicate with you and show you who you are and how to live for Him?

I'm so glad God looks at the intention of our hearts before He passes judgment. I'm thrilled that He declares that there is *no* condemnation to those who are in Christ Jesus (Romans 8:1). *Our* righteousness is through *His* righteousness—"even the righteousness of God, through faith in Jesus Christ, to all and on all who believe" (Romans 3:22).

Righteousness is a gift by God's grace to His people. Without salvation, we can't beg, borrow, barter, steal, or claim righteousness.

So here's the most crucial invitation of your life. If you haven't accepted Jesus Christ as your personal Lord and Savior, why not do it now? Express your confession that you know you're a sinner. You know that sinners without repentance cannot enter into heaven to live with the Lord when they die. If you want Jesus to live inside your heart now, you only have to ask Him. You can pray:

> *Dear Lord, I know I've done wrong. I want You to live in me and walk with me. Please come into my heart and cleanse me of all evil. Thank You for answering this prayer. Amen.*

That's it. If you sincerely prayed that, you just "got saved"! Wasn't it painless? Jesus took all your sins and pushed the delete button on His holy computer. He instantly cleaned your contaminated heart and replaced it with a heart of righteousness.

Scriptures of Joy and Hope

The following scriptures from the English Standard Version of the Bible will guide you in seeking, acknowledging, and experiencing God's righteousness.

- The law of the LORD is perfect, reviving the soul; the testimony of the LORD is sure, making wise the simple; the precepts of the LORD are right, rejoicing the heart; the commandment of the LORD is pure, enlightening the eyes; the fear of the LORD is clean, enduring forever; the rules of the LORD are true, and *righteous* altogether (Psalm 19:7-9).

- [God,] send out your light and your truth; let them lead me; let them bring me to your holy hill and to your dwelling! (Psalm 43:3).

- I have stored up your word in my heart, that I might not sin against you (Psalm 119:11).

- Your testimonies are my delight; they are my counselors (Psalm 119:24).

- Your word is a lamp to my feet and a light to my path (Psalm 119:105).

- The unfolding of your words gives light; it imparts understanding to the simple (Psalm 119:130).

- For as the rain and the snow come down from heaven and do not return there but water the earth, making it bring forth and sprout, giving seed to the sower and bread to the eater, so shall my word be that goes out from my mouth; it shall not return to me empty, but it shall accomplish that which I purpose, and shall succeed in the thing for which I sent it (Isaiah 55:10-11).

- It is the Spirit who gives life; the flesh is no avail. The words that I have spoken to you are spirit and life (John 6:63).

- Jesus said to the Jews who had believed in him, "If you abide in my word, you are truly my disciples, and you will know the truth, and the truth will set you free" (John 8:31-32).

- All Scripture is breathed out by God and profitable for teaching, for reproof, for correction, and for training in *righteousness*, that the man of God may be competent, equipped for every good work (2 Timothy 3:17).

- For the word of God is living and active, sharper than any two-edged sword, piercing to the division of soul and of spirit, of joints and of marrow, and discerning the thoughts and intentions of the heart (Hebrews 4:12).

- Having purified your souls by your obedience to the truth for a sincere brotherly love, love one another earnestly from a pure heart, since you have been born again, not of perishable seed but of imperishable, through the living and abiding word of God (1 Peter 1:22-23).

- His divine power has granted to us all things that pertain to life and godliness, through the knowledge of him who called us to his own glory and excellence, by which he has granted to us his precious and very great promises, so that through them you may become partakers of the divine nature, having escaped from the corruption that is in the world because of sinful desire (2 Peter 1:3-4).

And look at what these scriptures from the New King James Version say about righteousness and a clean heart.

- You will *seek* the LORD your God, and you will find Him if you *seek* Him with all your *heart* and with all your soul. When you are in distress, and all these things come upon you in the latter days, when you turn to the LORD your God and obey His voice (for the LORD your God is a merciful God), He will not forsake you nor destroy you, nor forget the covenant of your fathers which He swore to them (Deuteronomy 4:29-31).

- The LORD searches all *hearts* and understands all the intent of the thoughts. If you *seek* Him, He will be found by you; but if you forsake Him, He will cast you off forever (1 Chronicles 28:9).

- Blessed be the LORD, because He has heard the voice of my supplications! The LORD is my strength and my shield; my *heart* trusted in Him, and I am helped; therefore my *heart* greatly rejoices, and with my song I will praise Him (Psalm 28:6-7).

- When I kept silent, my bones grew old through my groaning all the day long. For day and night Your hand was heavy upon me; my vitality was turned into the drought of summer. I acknowledged my sin to You, and my iniquity I have not hidden. I said, "I will confess my transgressions to the LORD," and You forgave the iniquity of my sin (Psalm 32:3-5).

- He who trusts in the LORD, mercy shall surround him. Be glad in the LORD and rejoice, you *righteous*; and shout for joy, all you upright in *heart!* (Psalm 32:10-11).

- Create in me a clean *heart*, O God, and renew a steadfast spirit within me. Do not cast me away from Your presence, and do not take Your Holy Spirit from me. Restore to me the joy of Your salvation, and uphold me by Your generous Spirit (Psalm 51:10-12).

- In God is my salvation and my glory; the rock of my strength, and my refuge, is in God. Trust in Him at all times, you people; pour out your *heart* before Him; God is a refuge for us (Psalm 62:7-8).

- The *righteous* shall be glad in the LORD, and trust in Him. And all the upright in *heart* shall glory (Psalm 64:10).

- Trust in the LORD with all your *heart*, and lean not on your own understanding; in all your ways acknowledge Him, and He shall direct your paths (Proverbs 3:5-6).

- The path of the just is like the shining sun, that shines ever brighter unto the perfect day (Proverbs 4:18).

- Keep your *heart* with all diligence, for out of it spring the issues of life. Put away from you a deceitful mouth, and put perverse lips far from you. Let your eyes look straight ahead, and your eyelids look right before you. Ponder the path of your feet, and let all your ways be established. Do not turn to the right or the left; remove your foot from evil (Proverbs 4:20-27).

- [Jesus] was wounded for our transgressions, He was bruised for our iniquities; the chastisement for our peace was upon Him, and by His stripes we are healed. All we like sheep have gone astray; we have turned, every one, to his own way; and the LORD has laid on Him the iniquity of us all (Isaiah 53:5-6).

- The *heart* is deceitful above all things, and desperately wicked; who can know it? I, the LORD, search the *heart*, I test the mind, even to give every man according to his ways, according to the fruit of his doings (Jeremiah 17:9-10).

- "Now, therefore," says the LORD, "turn to Me with all your *heart*, with fasting, with weeping, and with mourning." So rend your *heart*, and not your garments; return to the LORD your God, for He is gracious and merciful, slow to anger, and of great kindness; and He relents from doing harm (Joel 2:12-13).

- A good man out of the good treasure of his *heart* brings forth good; and an evil man out of the evil treasure of his *heart* brings forth evil. For out of the abundance of the *heart* his mouth speaks (Luke 6:45).

- You are already clean because of the word which I have spoken to you. Abide in Me, and I in you. As the branch cannot bear fruit of itself, unless it abides in the vine, neither can you, unless you abide in Me. I am the vine, you are the branches. He who abides in Me, and I in him, bears much fruit; for without Me you can do nothing (John 15:3-5).

- The *righteousness* of God apart from the law is revealed, being witnessed by the Law and the Prophets, even the *righteousness* of God, through faith in Jesus Christ, to all and on all who believe. For there is no difference; for all have sinned and fall short of the glory of God, being justified freely by His grace through the redemption that is in Christ Jesus, whom God set forth as a propitiation by His blood, through faith, to demonstrate His *righteousness*, because in His forbearance God had passed over the sins that were previously committed, to demonstrate at the present time His *righteousness*, that He might be just and the justifier of the one who has faith in Jesus (Romans 3:21-26).

- If you confess with your mouth the Lord Jesus and believe in your *heart* that God has raised Him from the dead, you will be saved. For with the *heart* one believes unto *righteousness*, and with the mouth confession is made unto salvation. For the Scripture says, "Whoever believes on Him will not be put to shame" (Romans 10:9-11).

- For He made Him who knew no sin to be sin for us, that we might become the *righteousness* of God in Him (2 Corinthians 5:21).

- Therefore, my beloved, as you have always obeyed, not as in my presence only, but now much more in my absence, work out your own salvation with fear and trembling; for it is God who works in you both to will and to do for His good pleasure (Philippians 2:12-13).

- Therefore, brethren, having boldness to enter the Holiest by the blood of Jesus...let us draw near [to God] with a true *heart* in full assurance of faith, having our *hearts* sprinkled from an evil conscience and our bodies washed with pure water. Let us hold fast the confession of our hope without wavering, for He who promised is faithful (Hebrews 10:19,22-23).

- Let us lay aside every weight, and the sin which so easily ensnares us, and let us run with endurance the race that is set before us, looking unto Jesus, the author and finisher of our faith, who for the joy that was set before Him endured the cross, despising the shame, and has sat down at the right hand of the throne of God (Hebrews 12:1-2).

- Do not despise the chastening of the LORD, nor be discouraged when you are rebuked by Him; for whom the LORD loves He chastens, and scourges every son whom He receives (Hebrews 12:5).

- Beware lest you also fall from your own steadfastness, being led away with the error of the wicked; but grow in the grace and knowledge of our Lord and Savior Jesus Christ (2 Peter 3:17-18).

- My little children, let us not love in word or in tongue, but in deed and in truth. And by this we know that we are of the truth, and shall assure our *hearts* before Him. For if our heart condemns us, God is greater than our heart, and knows all things. Beloved, if our heart does not condemn us, we have confidence toward God. And whatever we ask we receive from Him, because we keep His commandments and do those things that are pleasing in His sight. And this is His commandment: that we should believe on the name of His Son Jesus Christ and love one another...He who keeps His commandments abides in Him, and He in him. And by this we know that He abides in us, by the Spirit whom He has given us (1 John 3:18-24).

Keeping First Things First

The breastplate of righteousness is the protective covering over our hearts that keeps out the dangers of faulty emotions and the schemes and lies of Satan. When our hearts are clean of dirt and debris and from all unrighteousness, we can think, envision, touch, and taste the goodness of God and keep first things first. "Seek first the kingdom of God and His righteousness, and all these things shall be added to you" (Matthew 6:33).

Tightening
Our Girdles

A Girdle? Really?

When I think of girdles my mind immediately conjures tight underwear designed to hold parts of me in. And then my mind drifts to old Western movies where the saloon ladies wore lace-up corsets that made them look like they had the shape of an old Coke bottle. They would take the long, coarse laces on the corsets and pull them tight until they could barely breathe. Surely those things must have restricted their circulation!

Today's modern version of a girdle is supposed to have the same function, but I don't think they're constructed as mechanically as they were back in the Wild Wild West. The salon ladies at the shop where I get my hair done were quick to let me know that those days are over and spandex is in.

Girdles of any era are used to form, brace, protect, strengthen, and hold in place the stomach, back, and other parts of the lower body.

Be Prepared

Girdles are generally classified as a "woman's elasticized foundation garment or corset extending from the waist to the thigh." When you "gird" the girdle or belt around you, the function is to get ready for something; to prepare for conflict or vigorous activity. I remember wearing those uncomfortable "foundation garments" years ago. And I was always concerned about circulation issues. The girdle performed its function to mold and shape me so my clothes would fit properly, thus making me look more appealing. But the garment was creating illusion rather than presenting the honest truth. Had I not worn this garment, my clothes would have fit differently and presented a more accurate visual of how I'm built.

At a recent National Religious Broadcasters Convention in Nashville, I was asked to be a panelist for one of the sessions. One question presented was, "What is the difference between mainstream media and Christian media?"

After a few seconds of thought I explained how all of us are influenced by the media—especially mainstream media. The mainstream is fueled by what people want to hear and see at a particular time. It's a benchmark for what is important to us at a particular time. For example, television, talk radio, and print media all follow a similar pattern of reporting what is sensational or selling at the moment. Media stories vacillate from the war in the Middle East to celebrity antics, from what happens in prisons to the political climate. If a story sells, it's reported or talked about over and over until the public begins to talk about it—and even believe it, although it may not be true.

Pop culture also directs us in what we drive, where we live, and how we act. Social standing, career development, financial cravings, religious beliefs, and emotional temperament are mirrored by media fantasies and follies.

Christian media has an obligation and responsibility to point out our fantasies and follies and direct people to a heartfelt knowledge and acceptance of the *truth* of Jesus Christ. There's only one source of truth in the universe. This Truth has been a force in the world before its very foundation. Jesus was there when God spoke the world into being. He was there when Adam and Eve were made. He was there when Lucifer fell from heaven and beguiled Eve. He was there, though not yet fully revealed, during the Old Testament days. In the New Testament He was openly revealed as the Messiah of the world. Truth was revealed *in* Him, *by* Him, *through* Him, and *because of* Him. Jesus told us, "I am the way, the truth, the life. No one comes to the Father except through Me" (John 14:6).

How About You?

What is real truth to you? Are you swayed by trends that sweep the country? Does the truth *you* believe please God? The truth sets your spirit free (John 8:32). Is your spirit free?

No one understands all truth. We don't really know why babies die, why bad things happen to good people, why some people get healed and other people don't, why some people are born with birth defects, why the economy gets so out of control, why people can't live in unity, and why there's so much suffering. Our questions are endless. Total truth is beyond our human comprehension. We're told in Deuteronomy 29:29, "The secret things belong to the LORD our God, but those things which are revealed belong to us and to our children forever, that we may follow all the words of this law." *Truth* extends from honesty, good faith, and sincerity to hard facts and reality.

In fact, few people agree completely on what truth is or isn't.

How can we know the truth so we can embrace it and put it on like God's Word tells us? "Stand therefore, having girded your waist with truth" (Ephesians 6:14).

Truth can never be completely defined by you and me; it's defined only by the Truth Himself—Jesus, who is the way, the truth, and the life. The way to seek complete truth is to pursue Jesus.

What does the truth set us free from? From falling into the traps set by the ungodly society we live in and our old enemy the devil. Satan wants us to believe we're not worthy of God's love. We are set free from falling into pits of contaminated hearts and unclean lips. Free from worry and anxiety. Free from hopelessness and despair. Free from poverty and distress. Free to speak up for what is right. Free to have the courage to speak out against sin and injustice. Free to speak the Word of God over any situation. And free to trust God for victory.

The Whole Truth

When people go before a judge to give testimony, they're generally asked to promise to "tell the truth, the whole truth, and nothing but the truth, so help me God." If a witness lies on the stand, that person may be convicted of perjury and have to pay a fine, go to jail, or both.

In a court of law, truth has to be proven by the plaintiff *and* the defense. The burden of proof is on each of them to substantiate what they believe. The attorney who convinces the court or jury what the truth is usually wins the case. However, in some cases, instead of truth winning, a verdict may be determined by the eloquence and courtroom drama of the winning side. There may be pertinent evidence of truth that the court or jury was never privy to.

In our society we're faced with the challenge every day of being asked to prove that the truth is found only in Jesus. The fact is, the physical signs of truth are constantly being dismantled in the houses of government, religion, medicine, business, and education. The sounds of truth are being hushed.

We've long enjoyed the freedom to worship as we choose and join any churches without reprisal, but today criticism is growing when God's truth confronts beliefs the world wants to embrace. So often biblical teaching is misinterpreted and the worship of God is watered down because of the intimidating tactics of those who fail to understand and accept the real Truth—Jesus Christ.

I believe the Holy Bible is the only source that can explain and reveal Truth in a way that we can understand. And part of that process is asking for the Holy Spirit's help. Let's put on the belt of truth:

> Gird up the loins of your mind, be sober, and rest your hope fully upon the grace that is to be brought to you at the revelation of Jesus Christ; as obedient children, not conforming yourselves to the former lusts, as in your ignorance; but as He who called you is holy, you also be holy in all your conduct, because it is written, "Be holy, for I am holy" (1 Peter 1:13-16).

Jesus Christ is the full revelation of God. *Truth* is mentioned twenty-two times in the Gospel of John alone. The first verses in John are an explanation of Jesus, revealing that He is the true and living Word of God:

> In the beginning was the Word, and the Word was with God, and the Word was God. He was in the beginning with God. All things came into being by Him, and apart from Him nothing came into being that has come into being (John 1:1-3 NASB).

Jesus has always existed, and everything depends on Him. Truth is the very principle of God. Truth is the backbone of creation. Truth is the revelation of all God is, all God has done, and all God will do. He cannot lie to us, disappoint us, forsake us, misrepresent us, fail us, cause us harm for harm's sake, or misguide us. All God's works are sustained by the blood of His Son and held up and given to us by the aid of the Holy Spirit. The truth is there is only one perfect entity of truth in the world, and it's the Trinity—God the Father, Jesus the Son, and the Holy Spirit, our guide.

Truth as Part of Our Armor

In the times of the Bible, soldiers wore a wide leather belt that was used to carry items, including their swords. The belt of truth represents a life and mind that is pulled together and ready to serve for the glory of God. The belt speaks to integrity, to truth in our inner beings.

Satan fights with lies, and sometimes his lies sound so much like truth. Christians have God's truth, and only that can successfully reveal Satan's lies. Mainstream culture does not have answers to the world's problems. By looking around us, it's evident others haven't cornered the truth because the world is confused and dismayed by what's going on—poverty, death, decay, crimes, debauchery, and so forth. Christians need to realize that the only truth is in Christ Jesus. The only hope we have is in Christ Jesus. With that in mind, how can we stand idly by and allow nontruths to spread like cancer throughout our nation and the world?

The charge to share the truth is found in the "Great Commission," in Matthew 28:19: "Go...and make disciples...baptizing them...teaching them to observe all things that I [Jesus] have commanded you." Yes, we're to go into the entire world and preach the gospel—the Good News—to every person in every nation. We can't compromise! The Spirit of truth must have full reign in our lives so we can help extend that reign to others. What a privilege for us! Jesus calls the Holy Spirit "the Spirit of truth, whom the world cannot receive, because it neither sees Him nor knows Him." Then He adds, "But you know Him, for He dwells with you and will be in you" (John 14:17). What a thrilling truth!

And Jesus encourages us, "When the Helper comes, whom I shall send to you from the Father, *the Spirit of truth* who proceeds from the Father, He will testify of Me" (John 15:26).

God's Truth

Before we can preach and teach the truth, we must know what the Bible says about the truth of God. Here is a small sampling of the wonderful truths we find in Scripture. These truths focus on the *totality* of who God is and what He has done. I've adapted this list from Elwin and Margit Roach's Pathfinder website:

49 Old Testament Truths

- Isaiah 46:10—God will do *all* His pleasure.
- Daniel 4:35—God's will done in heaven and earth, none can stop Him.
- Proverbs 16:9—Man devises, but God directs his steps.
- Proverbs 19:21—Man devises, but God's counsel stands.
- Proverbs 16:33—The whole disposing thereof is of the Lord.
- Psalm 37:23—The steps of man are ordered of God.
- Psalm 33:10—The LORD bringeth the counsel and devices of the heathen and the people to naught and of none effect.
- Psalm 33:15—God fashions *all* hearts.
- Job 5:17-18—God wounds then He makes whole.
- Hosea 6:1-2—God tears, but in the third day He heals.
- Deuteronomy 32:39—God kills and makes alive, He wounds but then heals.
- Psalm 90:3—God turns man to destruction, then says return.
- Jeremiah 18:2-6—God mars vessels and then remakes them.
- Lamentations 3:31-32—God will not cast off forever.
- Psalm 102:18-20—God will loosen those appointed to death.
- Isaiah 2:2—All nations will flow to the Lord's house.

- Joel 3:21—God will cleanse blood not cleansed.

- Genesis 18:18—All families of the earth will be blessed.

- Isaiah 45:22—All the earth commanded to look and be saved.

- Isaiah 45:23—To God *all* will bow and every tongue swear.

- Isaiah 40:3-5—Highway of God enables all flesh to see His glory.

- Psalm 138:4—All kings will praise God.

- Psalm 72:17—All nations will call Him blessed.

- Psalm 86:9—All nations will worship God and all men blessed.

- Isaiah 52:10—All earth will see the salvation of God.

- Psalm 65:2-4—All flesh will come to God.

- Isaiah 11:9—The earth will be full of the knowledge of the Lord.

- Psalm 66:3-4—Enemies will submit and all earth will worship.

- Isaiah 19:14-25—Egypt and Assyria will be restored.

- Ezekiel 16:55—Sodom will be restored.

- Psalm 68:18—God will lead captivity captive and dwell in man.

- Isaiah 54:5—He will be called the God of the whole earth.

- Psalm 22:25-29—All will remember and turn to the Lord.

- Psalm 145:9-10—God is good to all and merciful to His works.

- Psalm 145:14—Raises all that fall and all that be bowed down.

- Psalm 145:15—Eyes of all wait upon God, and He gives them meat in due season.

- Psalm 145:16—The Lord will satisfy desire of all living.

- Psalm 145:9—The Lord is good to all.

- Psalm 145:10—All God's works shall praise Him.

- Psalm 24:1—The Earth is the Lord's and the *fullness* thereof, and they who dwell therein.

- Isaiah 25:6—The Lord will make unto all people a feast.

- Isaiah 25:7—He will destroy the veil that's cast over all.

- Isaiah 25:8—He will swallow up death in victory.

- Isaiah 25:8—He will wipe away tears from all faces.

- Jeremiah 32:35—It never entered His mind to pass sons and daughters through the fire of Molech.

- Psalm 135:6—The Lord did what pleased Him in heaven, earth, and the sea.

- Isaiah 26:9—When God's judgments are in the earth, the inhabitants will learn righteousness.

- Isaiah 53:11—He shall see of the travail of His soul and shall be satisfied.

- Genesis 12:3—All families of the earth shall be blessed.

53 New Testament Truths

- Ephesians 1:11—God works all things after the counsel of His will.

- John 8:29—Jesus always does that which pleases His Father.

- 1 Timothy 2:4—God wants all to be saved.

- 1 John 4:14—Jesus sent to be the Savior of the world.

- John 4:34—Jesus to do the will of God who sent Him.

- John 12:47—Jesus came to save all.

- 1 Timothy 2:6—Jesus gave Himself as a ransom for all.

- John 5:36—He will finish the works He was sent to do.

- John 4:42—Jesus is the Savior of the world.

- John 12:32—Jesus will draw all to Himself.

- Hebrews 7:25—Jesus is able to save to the uttermost.

- Colossians 1:15—Jesus was the firstborn of all creation.

- Colossians 1:16—By Him all things were created.

- Romans 5:15-21—In Adam all condemned; in Christ all live.

- 1 Corinthians 15:22—In Adam all die; in Christ all live.

- Ephesians 1:10—All come into Him at the fullness of times.

- 1 Corinthians 15:26—Death, the last enemy, will be destroyed.

- Philippians 2:9-11—Every tongue shall confess Jesus is Lord.

- 1 Corinthians 12:3—No one can confess Jesus is Lord except by the Holy Spirit.

- Romans 11:26—All Israel will be saved.

- Act 3:20-21—Restitution (reconstitution) of all.

- Luke 2:10—Jesus will be joy to all people.

- Ephesians 2:7—His grace will be shown in the ages to come.

- Hebrews 8:11-12—All will know God.

- Luke 3:6—All flesh shall see the salvation of God.

- Titus 2:11—Grace has appeared to all.

- Romans 8:19-21—Creation freed from corruption.

- Colossians 1:20—All reconciled to God.

- 1 Corinthians 4:5—All will have praise of God.

- James 5:11—The Lord is full of mercy.

- Revelation 15:4—All nations worship when judgments seen.

- 2 Corinthians 5:17—All become new creations in Christ.

- Romans 11:32—All subjected to unbelief; God's mercy on all.

- Romans 11:36—All out of God, through Him, and into Him.

- Ephesians 4:10—Jesus will fill all things.

- Revelation 5:13—All creation praises God.

- 1 Corinthians 15:28—God will be all in all.

- Revelation 21:4-5—No more tears; all things made new.

- John 5:25—All dead who hear will live.

- John 5:28—All in the grave will hear and come forth.

- John 6:39—And this is the Father's; I should lose nothing.

- 1 Corinthians 3:15—All saved, yet dross gone via fire.

- Mark 9:49—Everyone shall be seasoned with fire.

- 2 Corinthians 5:15—Jesus died for all.

- 1 John 2:2—Jesus is the propitiation for the sins of the whole world.

- Romans 11:15—Reconciliation of the world.

- Hebrews 2:2—He is the heir of all things.

- John 3:35—All has been given into His hand.

- John 17:2—Jesus will give eternal life to all that His Father gives Him.

- John 6:44-45—All to be taught of God; everyone who hears and learns will come.

- 1 Timothy 4:9-11—Jesus is the Savior of all.

- Acts 13:47—Salvation unto the ends of the earth.

- Galatians 3:8—All nations shall be blessed.[1]

The Best Way to Discover Truth

The only real truth in the world is the truth that comes from the heart of God. Following any other alleged truth will mislead and confuse. It can be difficult to distinguish fact from fallacy. The more we discover what the Bible says about truth, the better we can keep on the path of truth.

Fasten God's truth in your heart and mind so you won't sin against God.

Remember: The *truth* is that our battle against our enemy has already been won! So don't wait to rejoice in the Lord. Do it now!

12

Putting on Our Stomping Shoes

*C*an you imagine how energized my conversation with the hair stylists at Salon Charis about dressing spiritually became when "put on stomping shoes" came up? Do you realize how many women buy several pairs of shoes to go with one outfit? I wonder how many people hoard shoes. I'm guilty. I believe that if I just hold on to my out-of-date shoes long enough they'll come back in style and I'll be ahead of the game. But that's shameful when there are people in this world who don't even have shoes to wear. Okay, I'm scolding myself for being selfish about shoes. This looks like an area I need to submit to the Lord and repent about. I'll do it right this minute. The minute we *know* right is when we should *do* right.

Father God, in the name of Your Son, Jesus, You know how I feel about my shoes. I admit I've been hoarding them and accumulating more and more. Father, as much as I'm not emotionally ready to give up some of my shoes, I ask You to regulate my mind and fix my heart to be obedient to Your commands. I repent of my selfishness, and I will immediately inventory my shoes. All those I don't wear and don't need, I will give to someone or some organization that will put them to good use by giving them to people who need them. Please forgive me, Lord, for being selfish. Help me realize when it's time to part with possessions. Thank You for Your mercy and grace. In Jesus' name I pray. Amen.

About Shoes

Footware varies from simple flip-flops to complex boots. Shoes may have high or low heels, although in Western cultures high heels are usually considered a woman's style. Materials for shoes include leather, canvas, plastics, cloth, rubber, and more.

When we cover our feet with shoes, we're protecting them from dangerous items such as nails or sharp rocks. We also get better traction on slippery surfaces. Shoes are barriers to the elements—heat, cold, rain, and snow. And shoes can help make us look spiffy.

Shoes can be dressy with plenty of bling-bling or plain, utilitarian, or unnoticeable. They come in every color under the sun. Heels vary from no heels to heels too tall for any person to walk in without the possibility of serious injury. But no matter what they look like, shoes are still shoes with the same basic functions. They're to be worn on our feet for safety and style.

Shhhh! Here comes a secret. I hide things in shoes. If you're playing a game that requires hiding something, what better place to hide an object than in a shoe? And I've got another idea for you. You may think I'm a bit wacky (and I might be), but I put Scripture in the inner soles of my children's and grandchildren's shoes as a symbol of them carrying the Word of God with them all the time and that the devil is under their feet because of Jesus. My husband and I also taught our children to hide God's Word in their hearts so they won't sin against God.

Our Feet and the Gospel

Our feet are to be "fitted with the readiness that comes from the gospel of peace" (Ephesians 6:15 NIV). Are you familiar with the Great Commission found in Matthew 28? When was the last time you put feet on your faith and told someone about the saving, peace-giving power of Jesus? Jesus said,

> Go therefore and make disciples of all nations, baptizing them in the name of the Father and of the Son and of the Holy Spirit, teaching them to observe all things that I have commanded you.

Are you intimidated about telling people you're a Christian? If so, does this fear please God?

Shoes for a Soldier

Soldiers must have sturdy, strong, durable shoes to stand on unstable ground and shaky ground. They must run or march over all types of terrain, from asphalt to desert sands, from swampy marshland to thick and tangled jungles. Soldiers must always be ready to move out quickly, and the right foot gear can make or break a battle or campaign.

Paul talks about the right foot gear for soldiers in Ephesians 6:15: "having shod your feet with the preparation of the gospel of peace." This means being ready to go and win. Warriors must go on the offense and also defend their positions. This preparedness takes training. Every soldier needs to toughen up enough to match the stamina of the others once their training is complete.

Just as the soldiers in the army are prepared, we too must be prepared as members of the army of the Lord. We must be ready and able at all times to defend our position in the Lord. To stand up for right. To fight the good fight of faith in a wicked and perverse world. When our feet are shod with the knowledge of the gospel of peace we're ready to tell the world about Jesus and His love for us. We'll go anywhere to spread the Good News—the gospel of Jesus Christ. Satan wants us to believe we're wasting time when we tell other people about Jesus. The devil wants us to believe the job is too big and any negative responses are too much for us to handle. But he is a liar!

When Jesus sent out seventy-two disciples in ministry, He said, "He who listens to you listens to me; he who rejects you rejects me; but he who rejects me rejects him who sent me." When these disciples "returned with joy" from their ministries, they reported, "Lord, even the demons submit to us in your name." Then Jesus replied,

> I saw Satan fall like lightning from heaven. I have given you authority to trample on snakes and scorpions and to overcome all the power of the enemy; nothing will harm you. However, do not rejoice that the spirits submit to you, but rejoice that your names are written in heaven (Luke 10:16-18 NIV).

As soldiers in the army of the Lord, we're called and motivated to share the true peace available through Jesus Christ. This is news that everyone needs to hear. Part of our training requires knowing the manual: "Be diligent to present yourself approved to God, a worker who does not need to be ashamed, rightly dividing the word of truth" (2 Timothy 2:15). The Bible, the inerrant Word of God, is the only written record containing all truth. It has stood—and will stand—stable, sturdy, and strong until the end of time. Every question we have, every desire we want, all the documentation we need, all the declarations of power, all the covenants we accept, each word of deliverance, signs and wonders to look for, and all the promises of God—they're contained in this mighty Book. Using the authority of God's Word combined with personal life experiences, we have all the ammunition we need to change the world for Christ and fight the good fight of faith to become victors over enemies.

Paul's encouragement to young Timothy, applies to us too:

- Never be ashamed of bearing witness to our Lord, nor of me [Paul], his prisoner. Accept your share of the hardship that faithfulness to the Gospel entails in the strength that God gives you. For he has saved us from all that is evil and called us to a life of holiness—not because of any of our achievements but for his own purpose. Before time began he planned to give us in Christ Jesus the grace to achieve this purpose, but it is only since our saviour Christ Jesus has been revealed that the method has become apparent. For Christ has completely abolished death, and has now, through the Gospel, opened to us…the shining possibilities of the life that is eternal (2 Timothy 1:8-10 PHILLIPS).

- Remember always, as the centre of everything, Jesus Christ, a descendant of David, yet raised by God from the dead according to my gospel. For preaching this I am having to endure being chained in prison as if I were some sort of a criminal. But they cannot chain the Word of God, and I can endure all these things for the sake of those whom God is calling, so that they too may receive the salvation of Christ Jesus, and its complement of glory after the world of time. I rely on this saying: If we died with him we shall also live with him: if we endure we shall also reign with him. If we deny him he will also deny us: yet if we are faithless he always remains faithful. He cannot deny his own nature (2:8-13).

- You [Timothy] must realise that in the last days [before the return of Jesus] the times will be full of danger [from evil men and false prophets] (3:1-2).

- [Remember] how from early childhood your mind has been familiar with the holy scriptures, which can open the mind to the salvation which comes through believing in Christ Jesus. All scripture is inspired by God and is useful for teaching the faith and correcting error, for re-setting the direction of a man's life and training him in good living. The scriptures are the comprehensive equipment of the man of God and fit him fully for all branches of his work (3:15-17).

Note also what these scriptures teach about the gospel and our mission:

- [Jesus] said to them, "Go into all the world and preach the gospel to every creature" (Mark 16:15).

- Preach the word! Be ready in season and out of season. Convince, rebuke, exhort, with all longsuffering and teaching (2 Timothy 4:2).

- This gospel of the kingdom will be preached in all the world as a witness to all the nations, and then the end will come (Matthew 24:14).

- In vain they worship Me [Jesus], teaching as doctrines the commandments of men (Mark 7:7).

- Be even more diligent to make your call and election sure, for if you do these things you will never stumble (2 Peter 1:10).

- Work hard to prove that you really are among those God has called and chosen. Do these things, and you will never fall away. Then God will give you a grand entrance into the eternal Kingdom of our Lord and Savior Jesus Christ (2 Peter 1:10-11 NLT).

- Indeed the gospel was preached to us as well as to them [the people Moses led out of Egypt]; but the word which they heard did not profit them, not being mixed with faith in those who heard it (Hebrews 4:2).

- "But the word of the Lord endures forever." Now this is the word which by the gospel was preached to you (1 Peter 1:25).

Wanting to Dance

There's one last function of the shoes of the gospel of peace that we want to enjoy. Shoes were made for dancing too! When we've got the joy of the Lord in our hearts—that joy that the world doesn't give, and that the world can't take away—we want to *dance* with elation. When the Spirit of Peace and the good news of the gospel fills my heart, I want to praise Him! I want to dance like David danced! "David danced before the LORD with all his might" (2 Samuel 6:14).

One Sunday morning I was having my private time with the Lord in the bathtub. I was listening to praise music, praising Him, and praying. The joy of the Lord was upon me, and when I got out of the tub, still soaking wet, I danced. My husband was on the other side of the house and heard me singing with energy and enthusiasm so he came to see what was going on.

"What are you doing?" he asked.

I told him the Spirit of the Lord was upon me, and I had the urge to dance before the Lord just as I was right that minute. And then I asked him to dance with me. On that beautiful Sunday morning just before I got ready for Sunday school, my husband and I waltzed before the Lord and honored Him with our holy praise.

Singing and dancing before God opens the portals of heaven so God receives our joyful and humble praise. He anoints us (prepares us) to tell people about His goodness and what Jesus did for us. Can't you just picture God pouring out His joy on us by dancing over us and spinning like a top around us? I can!

We who have experienced the awesomeness of our wonderful Savior understand the Good News of the gospel isn't to be kept to ourselves; it is not to be hoarded like shoes in our closets. So we joyfully and excitedly tell it on the mountains, over the hills, and everywhere that Jesus Christ was born, suffered, bled, died, and rose from the grave to set us free from eternal damnation! With a spring in our steps and sweet rhythm in our hearts we rejoice that when we die, we pass from this life to a new life in Him where our joy will never wane or end. No suffering and pain; no poverty and shame; no problems to face. Death is not the end of living. Those who accept Jesus Christ will live with Him in glory forever!

But those who don't know Jesus or don't accept Him will live in torment that will never end. So it's imperative that we tell people about Jesus! He loves them and wants them to know the truth. They need to know there's no friend like Jesus who sticks closer than a brother. They need to know that when they accept Jesus as their personal Savior and Lord, the Holy Spirit comes to live within their hearts. And from then on they will be guided by the Spirit of God.

This is a serious obligation and responsibility. Though they may not believe us or want to hear our message, we must tell them. So tell them. Don't worry about the results because God bears that burden. Some people plant *seeds of salvation*. Other people emphasize the *need for salvation*. And still others are living witnesses of the *power of salvation*. God will draw all people to Him if they're willing to open their hearts and let Jesus in.

Praise the Lord!

Our preparation for battle is the gospel of Jesus Christ. With the Word of God we have our instructions on how to fight. Only those who know the general (Jesus) in the army of God fight fearlessly and courageously with the assuredness of victory. We don't have to worry about *how* we'll win; we have faith and trust in God that the battle is won before it's begun.

Thank you, Lord, for sending Jesus to save us! Come and sing with me!

Just as I am—without one plea,
But that Thy blood was shed for me,
And that Thou bidst me come to Thee,
O Lamb of God, I come!

Just as I am—poor, wretched, blind;
Sight, riches, healing of the mind,
Yea, all I need, in Thee to find,
O Lamb of God, I come!

Just as I am—and waiting not
To rid my soul of one dark blot,
To Thee, whose blood can cleanse each spot,
O Lamb of God, I come!

Just as I am—Thy love, I own,
Has broken every barrier down;
Now to be Thine, my joy and crown,
O Lamb of God, I come!

Just as I am—of that free love
the fullness and the depth to prove,
Here for a season, then above—
O Lamb of God, I come![1]

13

Grabbing Our Shields and Swords

There's a joke among some of my friends about my hair. They have hair that they just seem to shake and it gets dry. Well, Sweetie, I can shake my wet hair too, but it won't get dry or be straight. Oh no…it draws up really short and swells up like somebody whacked it. It was hit all right, but not by a person. Whether it's water from the shower or a shower of rain, my hair gets out of control. So my motto is, "I don't get my hair wet when I'm out and about." I'll let my shoes, clothes, and purse get soaked before I'll let my hair even get damp. I've been known to sit in a car or on a bus until the rain stops or somebody brings me a secure covering for my head.

I've taken to carrying a rain cap with me everywhere I go. Once I got caught without it after church one Sunday. I was determined to stay in the building until the rain stopped…just because of my hair. I wasn't going to let it get wet. Looking back, *now* I think this is funny. Unfortunately my plan didn't work because everybody was leaving, and the people in charge wanted to lock up the building.

One of my friends finally came up with some newspapers to cover my hairdo. Because my car was parked a good distance from the front door, I still got wet—and my hair turned into a furry beach ball. If I were a grouchy person I would've been out of sorts the rest of the day. It's a good thing I'm not!

Why this big discussion on a simple subject like wet hair? My rain cap is a shield against my hair getting wet, so, like I said, I make sure I have one handy all the time. Even when the sun is shining I feel uneasy if I don't have my shield stashed nearby. In fact, I've been known to go home and get it just like I do when I forget my cell phone.

Hmmm...now that I think about it, I really depend on this rain cap every day and in all kinds of weather just so I'll *feel* safe and protected. That physical and emotional dependency can drift into obsession. In fact, I'm glad I'm writing this chapter because I've never thought about being paranoid about getting wet enough to become dependent on a little piece of plastic with a string sewed on to tie around my chin.

I think from now on I'll continue to keep a rain cap in my purse, but I'm going to view it differently. I'm going to change my emotional attachment. I'm going to think of it as my shield...a representative of the shield of faith. Doesn't that sound great? I'll be continually reminded to grab one of the defenses God gives us against the wiles of the devil. When I dress spiritually every morning I lightly rub oil on my body with anointing oil to symbolically pick up my shield of faith: "[Grab] the shield of faith with which you will be able to quench all the fiery darts of the wicked one" (Ephesians 6:16). And a logical adjunct is the sword of the Spirit— God's Word.

Roman soldiers soaked their wooden and leather shields overlaid with metal in water before going into battle so the defensive tool would keep them from being skewered or arrowed, but it also put out the fiery darts hurled at them by enemies. You and I are in a daily battle too. We fight the temptations of this world. Every minute of every day Satan and his cohorts are committed to hitting us where they hope we're unprotected.

For instance, we've all had days where we woke up "on the wrong side of the bed." We're short and abrupt with our families and determined to stay that way all day...just because. We've set our attitude for the day before we even figured out what we were going to be doing. But if we wake up and pray and get dressed and grab our shields and swords, we let God and our faith set up our day.

Another example is when we let a negative event in the past haunt us. We continually replay the scenes, which frustrate us and cause us to focus on the negative. If we go shopping and someone stands too close to us in the check-out stand, we become irritated, roll our eyes, and either silently suffer or snap at the person. But if we have our shields in place, we can ward off the irritation and talk to God about the situation.

We've all been given a measure of faith, but what we do with the measure is completely up to us. When we interact with people and circumstances, we can illustrate our faith in the power of Christ and share His truth (our swords) or we can lower our shields and succumb to the attacks. What is *faith* for the Christian? According to my dictionary, faith is "the theological virtue defined as secure belief in God and a trusting acceptance of God's will." For a Christian, faith is a way of life. It's the acceptance of what we can't see but what we feel deep within our spirits. Faith is the belief (and knowledge!) that one day we'll stand before our Lord and Savior, Jesus Christ, and live with Him forever.

At many of my speaking engagements I begin by reciting Romans 1:16-17: "I am not ashamed of the gospel of Christ, for it is the power of God to salvation for everyone who believes, for the Jew first and also for the Greek. For in it the righteousness of God is revealed from faith to faith; as it is written, 'The just shall live by faith.'" I believe that with all my heart. I am justified by God through Jesus Christ, and that happened the moment I asked Jesus to be Lord and Savior of my life. Since I know faith is the righteous shield that can cover me completely and keep me safe from temptation and the wiles of the devil, what's the problem? Well, I'm sure you can relate. Often when I'm hurt, being questioned, disappointed, interrupted, delayed, talked down to, teased, or ridiculed I forget that I have protection and all I have to do is raise my shield and use the sword of the Spirit (Truth!).

Fortunately I've discovered one sure thing: If I forget I'm covered and protected by the faith I have in God and by His faithfulness to me, I can do what I do when I get caught out in the rain without a hat. I can stop, grab my shield, hold it up, and adjust my attitude by keeping my tongue quiet, starting over, and thanking God that He's given me His shield of protection. To remember to do this, I need to be rooted and grounded in the fact that the shield of faith is part of the armor I received when I accepted Jesus. It stays attached to me in all circumstances and covers me in spite of me. And I need to keep God's truth close by wielding the sword of the Spirit.

Every eight seconds, when I bat my eyes, I can look back over my life and see how God has protected me from emotionalism and taking the fight against the devil and temptation into my own hands. I need to remember that the battles of life are not mine to deal with unprotected. No! I am protected by the shield of faith and the sword of truth—and so are you. We live in a protective bubble where nobody and nothing can attack us successfully. It's only when we burst the bubble or step out of the bubble that we get vulnerable.

Don't Live Unprotected

Won't you join me in deciding to become more alert, more discerning, and more mindful of our position in Jesus through faith? We can look to God for our weapons and defenses. We can look back over the faith of our fathers and grab hold of that which sustained them for decades. Lasting faith always protects, always perseveres, always wins, is not found in silver, wood, precious stones, our eloquence, our education, our finances, or our community. True and powerful faith is in Jesus. And by joining with fellow believers we are strengthened in our faith and stand hand in hand, arm to arm, thought to thought, commitment to commitment to win the battle against the enemy of our souls.

If people work together in harmony we can change the face of our nation, our families, and the world around us. Since we're going to fix our hair, pad our bras, tighten our girdles, and put on our stomping shoes, we also can't afford to leave home without our coats—our shields that cover us in the front, back, sides, arms, and legs and our swords that give us the truth to fight our enimies' lies. The shield of faith is life and death—far more important than a little ol' rain cap. If I get my hair wet (Eek!) I just have to let it dry and redo it to make it presentable. If I forget my shield of faith, I might be exposed to circumstances that often take time, maybe even a lifetime, to work out. And we need to take up God's Word, the sword of the spirit to remind us who we are, whose army we're in, and what we're doing.

Praise the Lord that we don't have to live unprotected any longer! We've got the blood of Jesus, the love of Jesus, the hope in Jesus, the restoration of Jesus, and the total covering by Him for our heads, hearts, minds, feet, and backs. We can stand strong in the midst of turmoil, ready to fight the good fight of faith without fear. Scripture says, "Above all, taking the shield of faith." Now that's an imperative!

Without faith it is impossible to please God and spiritual victory won't happen. Faith is the substance of things hoped for. Faith assures us that God hears and answers our prayers. Faith sparks our hope in the healing power of God. Faith gives us assurance that we will have what we need to live. Faith helps us hold on to the promises of God when things look bleak. Faith helps us deal with changes in climate and the uncertainties of life. Faith helps us lean on the everlasting arms of God when all around us is crashing. Faith reaches beyond what we can see and gives us encouragement that life will work out in the future.

Do you understand that without faith you can't please the Lord? Are you ready for attacks by the evil one? Is your faith solid and your mind made up to trust in the Lord with all your heart? Is your shield soaked in the powerful blood of the Lamb? Are you determined to hold to God's unchanging hands and hold on to the sword of the Spirit (the Bible) as the unwavering truth that can give you all the fighting instructions you need? I hope and pray your answer is yes!

You're Ready to Win!

Don't forget to prepare for the fight every morning:

- Fix your hair!
- Pad your bra!
- Tighten your girdle!
- Put on your stomping shoes!
- Grab your shield and sword!

Ammunition

The Bible is the voice of God, our source of truth and wisdom, and our guide to winning. Here's a list of scriptures from the New American Standard Bible to give you strength, encouragement, and ammunition as you fight the good fight of faith and be victorious over the devil.

Believe in God

- For God so loved the world, that He gave His only begotten Son, that whoever believes in Him shall not perish, but have eternal life (John 3:16).

- Of Him all the prophets bear witness that through His name everyone who believes in Him receives forgiveness of sins (Act 10: 43).

- It is written, "Behold, I lay in Zion a stone of stumbling and a rock of offense, and he who believes in Him will not be disappointed" (Romans 9:33).

- As many as received Him, to them He gave the right to become children of God, even to those who believe in His name (John 1:12).

- He who believes in [Jesus] is not judged; he who does not believe has been judged already, because he has not believed in the name of the only begotten Son of God (John 3:18).

- He who believes in the Son has eternal life; but he who does not obey the Son will not see life, but the wrath of God abides on him (John 3:36).

- Believe in the Lord Jesus, and you will be saved, you and your household (Acts 16:31).

- I [Jesus] have come as Light into the world, so that everyone who believes in Me will not remain in darkness (John 12:46).

- Jesus said to them, "I am the bread of life; he who comes to Me will not hunger, and he who believes in Me will never thirst" (John 6:35).

- Jesus said to him, " 'If You can?' All things are possible to him who believes" (Mark 9:23).

- Jesus said to him, "Because you have seen Me, have you believed? Blessed are they who did not see, and yet believed" (John 20:29).

- Truly, truly, I [Jesus] say to you, he who believes has eternal life (John 6:47).

- Now if we have died with Christ, we believe that we shall also live with Him (Romans 6:8).

- The Scripture has shut up everyone under sin, so that the promise by faith in Jesus Christ might be given to those who believe (Galatians 3:22).

- For if we believe that Jesus died and rose again, even so God will bring with Him those who have fallen asleep in Jesus (1 Thessalonians 4:14).

- For this reason I found mercy, so that in me as the foremost, Jesus Christ might demonstrate His perfect patience as an example for those who would believe in Him for eternal life (1 Timothy 1:16).

- This is His commandment, that we believe in the name of His Son Jesus Christ, and love one another, just as He commanded us (1 John 3:23).

- Now I desire to remind you, though you know all things once for all, that the Lord, after saving a people out of the land of Egypt, subsequently destroyed those who did not believe (Jude 5).

- For to you it has been granted for Christ's sake, not only to believe in Him, but also to suffer for His sake (Philippians 1:29).

God's Faithfulness

- You have dealt well with Your servant, O Lord, according to Your word (Psalm 119:65).

- Faithful is He who calls you, and He also will bring it to pass (1 Thessalonians 5:24).

- "For this is like the days of Noah to Me, when I swore that the waters of Noah would not flood the earth again; so I have sworn that I will not be angry with you nor will I rebuke you. For the mountains may be removed and the hills may shake, but My lovingkindness will not be removed from you, and My covenant of peace will not be shaken," says the Lord who has compassion on you (Isaiah 54:9-10).

- When the bow is in the cloud, then I will look upon it, to remember the everlasting covenant between God and every living creature of all flesh that is on the earth (Genesis 9:16).

- Behold, I am with you and will keep you wherever you go, and will bring you back to this land; for I will not leave you until I have done what I have promised you (Genesis 28:15).

- [Know] that the LORD your God, He is God, the faithful God, who keeps His covenant and His lovingkindness to a thousandth generation with those who love Him and keep His commandments (Deuteronomy 7:9).

- You know in all your hearts and in all your souls that not one word of all the good words which the LORD your God spoke concerning you has failed; all have been fulfilled for you, not one of them has failed (Joshua 23:14).

- Your lovingkindness, O LORD, extends to the heavens, Your faithfulness reaches to the skies (Psalm 36:5).

- I will sing of the lovingkindness of the LORD forever; to all generations I will make known Your faithfulness with my mouth. For I have said, "Lovingkindness will be built up forever; in the heavens You will establish Your faithfulness" (Psalm 89:1-2).

- But I will not break off My lovingkindness from him, nor deal falsely in My faithfulness. My covenant I will not violate, nor will I alter the utterance of My lips (Psalm 89:33-34).

- He will not allow your foot to slip; He who keeps you will not slumber (Psalm 121:3-4).

- God is faithful, through whom you were called into fellowship with His Son, Jesus Christ our Lord (1 Corinthians 1:9).

- No temptation has overtaken you but such as is common to man; and God is faithful, who will not allow you to be tempted beyond what you are able, but with the temptation will provide the way of escape also, so that you will be able to endure it (1 Corinthians 10:13).

- The Lord is not slow about His promise, as some count slowness, but is patient toward you, not wishing for any to perish but for all to come to repentance (2 Peter 3:9).

- If we are faithless, He remains faithful, for He cannot deny Himself...Nevertheless, the firm foundation of God stands, having this seal, "The Lord knows those who are His," and, "Everyone who names the name of the Lord is to abstain from wickedness" (2 Timothy 2:13,19).

God's Grace and Favor

- And with great power the apostles were giving testimony to the resurrection of the Lord Jesus, and abundant grace was upon them all (Acts 4:33).

- Do not let kindness and truth leave you...You will find favor and good repute in the sight of God and man (Proverbs 3:3-4).

- For the LORD God is a sun and shield; the LORD gives grace and glory; no good thing does He withhold from those who walk uprightly (Psalm 84:11).

- You have granted me life and lovingkindness; and Your care has preserved my spirit (Job 10:12).

- It is You who blesses the righteous man, O LORD, You surround him with favor as with a shield (Psalm 5:12).

- The LORD has been mindful of us; He will bless us; He will bless the house of Israel; He will bless the house of Aaron. He will bless those who fear the LORD, the small together with the great (Psalm 115:12-13).

- Blessings are on the head of the righteous, but the mouth of the wicked conceals violence...It is the blessing of the LORD that makes rich, and He adds no sorrow to it...What the wicked fears will come upon him, but the desire of the righteous will be granted (Proverbs 10:6,22,24).

- For all things are for your sakes, so that the grace which is spreading to more and more people may cause the giving of thanks to abound to the glory of God (2 Corinthians 4:15).

- To the praise of the glory of His grace, which He freely bestowed on us in the Beloved (Ephesians 1:6).

- Let us draw near with confidence to the throne of grace, so that we may receive mercy and find grace to help in time of need (Hebrews 4:16).

Our Hope and Faith

- Why are you in despair, O my soul? And why have you become disturbed within me? Hope in God, for I shall yet praise Him, the help of my countenance and my God (Psalm 42:11).

- [Jesus] has appeared in these last times for the sake of you who through Him are believers in God, who raised Him from the dead and gave Him glory, so that your faith and hope are in God (1 Peter 1:20-21).

- Prepare your minds for action, keep sober in spirit, fix your hope completely on the grace to be brought to you at the revelation of Jesus Christ (1 Peter 1:13).

- Beloved, now we are children of God…we know that when He appears, we will be like Him, because we will see Him just as He is. And everyone who has this hope fixed on Him purifies himself, just as He is pure (1 John 3:2-3).

- The wicked is thrust down by his wrongdoing, but the righteous has a refuge when he dies (Proverbs 14:32).

- God willed to make known what is the riches of the glory of this mystery among the Gentiles, which is Christ in you, the hope of glory (Colossians 1:27).

- Be strong and let your heart take courage, all you who hope in the LORD (Psalm 31:24).

- You are my hope; O Lord GOD, You are my confidence from my youth (Psalm 71:5).

- Blessed be the God and Father of our Lord Jesus Christ, who according to His great mercy has caused us to be born again to a living hope through the resurrection of Jesus Christ from the dead (1 Peter 1:3).

Trust in God

- Offer the sacrifices of righteousness, and trust in the LORD (Psalm 4:5).

- Those who know Your name will put their trust in You, for You, O LORD, have not forsaken those who seek You (Psalm 9:10).

- My God, in You I trust, do not let me be ashamed; do not let my enemies exult over me (Psalm 25:2).

- I trust in the LORD (Psalm 31:6).

- As for me, I trust in You, O Lord, I say, "You are my God" (Psalm 31:14).

- Our heart rejoices in Him, because we trust in His holy name (Psalm 33:21).

- Trust in the Lord and do good; dwell in the land and cultivate faithfulness (Psalm 37:3).

- Commit your way to the Lord, trust also in Him, and He will do it (Psalm 37:5).

- He put a new song in my mouth, a song of praise to our God; many will see and fear and will trust in the Lord. How blessed is the man who has made the Lord his trust, and has not turned to the proud, nor to those who lapse into falsehood (Psalm 40:3-4).

- I trust in the lovingkindness of God forever and ever (Psalm 52:8).

- When I am afraid, I will put my trust in You. In God, whose word I praise, in God I have put my trust; I shall not be afraid. What can mere man do to me? (Psalm 56:3-4).

- Trust in Him at all times, O people; pour out your heart before Him; God is a refuge for us (Psalm 62:8).

- Trust in the Lord with all your heart and do not lean on your own understanding (Proverbs 3:5).

- Trust in the Lord forever, for in God the Lord, we have an everlasting Rock (Isaiah 26:4).

Wait on the Lord

- My soul, wait in silence for God only, for my hope is from Him (Psalm 62:5).

- Our soul waits for the Lord; He is our help and our shield (Psalm 33:20).

- Let us hold fast the confession of our hope without wavering, for He who promised is faithful (Hebrews 10:23).

- For we have become partakers of Christ, if we hold fast the beginning of our assurance firm until the end (Hebrews 3:14).

- It will be said in that day, "Behold, this is our God for whom we have waited that He might save us. This is the LORD for whom we have waited; let us rejoice and be glad in His salvation" (Isaiah 25:9).

- Rest in the LORD and wait patiently for Him; do not fret because of him who prospers in his way, because of the man who carries out wicked schemes. Cease from anger and forsake wrath; do not fret; it leads only to evildoing. For evildoers will be cut off, but those who wait for the LORD, they will inherit the land (Psalm 37:7-9).

- I waited patiently for the LORD; and He inclined to me and heard my cry. He brought me up out of the pit of destruction, out of the miry clay, and He set my feet upon a rock making my footsteps firm. He put a new song in my mouth, a song of praise to our God; many will see and fear and will trust in the LORD (Psalm 40:1-3).

- The LORD longs to be gracious to you, and therefore He waits on high to have compassion on you. For the LORD is a God of justice; how blessed are all those who long for Him (Isaiah 30:18).

- None of those who wait for [God] will be ashamed; those who deal treacherously without cause will be ashamed. Make me know Your ways, O LORD; teach me Your paths. Lead me in Your truth and teach me, for You are the God of my salvation; for You I wait all the day (Psalm 25:3-5).

- Wait for the LORD; be strong and let your heart take courage; yes, wait for the LORD (Psalm 27:14).

- The LORD is good to those who wait for Him, to the person who seeks Him. It is good that he waits silently for the salvation of the LORD (Lamentations 3:25-26).

- As for me, I will watch expectantly for the LORD; I will wait for the God of my salvation. My God will hear me (Micah 7:7).

- My soul, wait in silence for God only, for my hope is from Him. He only is my rock and my salvation, my stronghold; I shall not be shaken (Psalm 62:5-6).

- The LORD sustains all who fall and raises up all who are bowed down. The eyes of all look to You, and You give them their food in due time (Psalm 145:14-15).

- Return to your God, observe kindness and justice, and wait for your God continually (Hosea 12:6).

The Wisdom of God

- But if any of you lacks wisdom, let him ask of God, who gives to all generously and without reproach, and it will be given to him (James 1:5).

- He will teach us His ways, and we shall walk in His paths (Isaiah 2:3).

- To a person who is good in His sight He has given wisdom and knowledge and joy (Ecclesiastes 2:26).

- I will bless the LORD who has counseled me; indeed, my mind instructs me in the night (Psalm 16:7).

- Then you will discern the fear of the LORD and discover the knowledge of God. For the LORD gives wisdom; from His mouth come knowledge and understanding. He stores up sound wisdom for the upright; He is a shield to those who walk in integrity (Proverbs 2:5-6).

- Behold, You desire truth in the innermost being, and in the hidden part You will make me know wisdom (Psalm 51:6).

- We know that the Son of God has come, and has given us understanding so that we may know Him who is true; and we are in Him who is true, in His Son Jesus Christ. This is the true God and eternal life (1 John 5:20).

- For God, who said, "Light shall shine out of darkness," is the One who has shone in our hearts to give the light of the knowledge of the glory of God in the face of Christ (2 Corinthians 4:6).

- Evil men do not understand justice, but those who seek the LORD understand all things (Proverbs 28:5).

Fight the Good Fight of Faith

- To this end also we pray for you always, that our God will count you worthy of your calling, and fulfill every desire for goodness and the work of faith with power, so that the name of our Lord Jesus will be glorified (2 Thessalonians 1:11-12).

- Simon, Simon, behold, Satan has demanded permission to sift you like wheat; but I [Jesus] have prayed for you, that your faith may not fail; and you, when you have turned again, strengthen your brothers (Luke 22:31-32).

- Let us lay aside the deeds of darkness and put on the armor of light. Let us behave properly as in the day, not in carousing and drunkenness, not in sexual promiscuity and sensuality, not in strife and jealousy. But put on the Lord Jesus Christ, and make no provision for the flesh (Romans 13:12-14).

- You were called to freedom, brethren; only do not turn your freedom into an opportunity for the flesh, but through love serve one another. For the whole Law is fulfilled in one word, in the statement, "YOU SHALL LOVE YOUR NEIGHBOR AS YOURSELF."...I say, walk by the Spirit, and you will not carry out the desire of the flesh. For the flesh sets its desire against the Spirit, and the Spirit against the flesh; for these are in opposition to one another, so that you may not do the things that you please. But if you are led by the Spirit, you are not under the Law.

  Now the deeds of the flesh are evident, which are: immorality, impurity, sensuality, idolatry, sorcery, enmities, strife, jealousy, outbursts of anger, disputes, dissensions, factions, envying, drunkenness, carousing, and things like these, of which I forewarn you, just as I have forewarned you, that those who practice such things will not inherit the kingdom of God. But the fruit of the Spirit is love, joy, peace, patience, kindness, goodness, faithfulness, gentleness, self-control; against such things there is no law. Now those who belong to Christ Jesus have crucified the flesh with its passions and desires. If we live by the Spirit, let us also walk by the Spirit (Galatians 5:13-14, 16-25).

- You were dead in your trespasses and sins, in which you formerly walked according to the course of this world, according to the prince of the power of the air, of the spirit that is now working in the sons of disobedience. Among them we too all formerly lived in the lusts of our flesh, indulging the desires of the flesh and of the mind, and were by nature children of wrath, even as the rest. But God, being rich in mercy, because of His great love with which He loved us, even when we were dead in our transgressions, made us alive together with Christ (by grace you have been saved), and raised us up with Him, and seated us with Him in the heavenly places in Christ Jesus (Ephesians 2:1-7).

- If indeed you have heard Him and have been taught in Him, just as truth is in Jesus, that, in reference to your former manner of life, you lay aside the old self, which is being corrupted in accordance with the lusts of deceit, and that you be renewed in the spirit of your mind, and put on the new self, which in the likeness of God has been created in righteousness and holiness of the truth. Therefore, laying aside falsehood, SPEAK TRUTH EACH ONE of you WITH HIS NEIGHBOR, for we are members of one another. BE ANGRY, AND yet DO NOT SIN; do not let the sun go down on your anger, and do not give the devil an opportunity.

  He who steals must steal no longer; but rather he must labor, performing with his own hands what is good, so that he will have something to share with one who has need. Let no unwholesome word proceed from your mouth, but only such a word as is good for edification according to the need of the moment, so that it will give grace to those who hear. Do not grieve the Holy Spirit of God, by whom you were sealed for the day of redemption. Let all bitterness and wrath and anger and clamor and slander be put away from you, along with all malice. Be kind to one another, tender-hearted, forgiving each other, just as God in Christ also has forgiven you (Ephesians 4:21-32).

- Be imitators of God, as beloved children; and walk in love, just as Christ also loved you and gave Himself up for us, an offering and a sacrifice to God as a fragrant aroma. But immorality or any impurity or greed must not even be named among you, as is proper among saints; and there must be no filthiness and silly talk, or coarse jesting, which are not fitting, but rather giving of thanks.

For this you know with certainty, that no immoral or impure person or covetous man, who is an idolater, has an inheritance in the kingdom of Christ and God.

Let no one deceive you with empty words, for because of these things the wrath of God comes upon the sons of disobedience. Therefore do not be partakers with them; for you were formerly darkness, but now you are Light in the Lord; walk as children of Light (for the fruit of the Light consists in all goodness and righteousness and truth), trying to learn what is pleasing to the Lord. Do not participate in the unfruitful deeds of darkness, but instead even expose them; for it is disgraceful even to speak of the things which are done by them in secret. But all things become visible when they are exposed by the light, for everything that becomes visible is light. For this reason it says, "Awake, sleeper, and arise from the dead, and Christ will shine on you." Therefore be careful how you walk, not as unwise men but as wise, making the most of your time, because the days are evil.

So then do not be foolish, but understand what the will of the Lord is. And do not get drunk with wine, for that is dissipation, but be filled with the Spirit, speaking to one another in psalms and hymns and spiritual songs, singing and making melody with your heart to the Lord; always giving thanks for all things in the name of our Lord Jesus Christ to God, even the Father; and be subject to one another in the fear of Christ (Ephesians 5:1-21).

• Flee from youthful lusts and pursue righteousness, faith, love and peace, with those who call on the Lord from a pure heart. But refuse foolish and ignorant speculations, knowing that they produce quarrels. The Lord's bond-servant must not be quarrelsome, but be kind to all, able to teach, patient when wronged, with gentleness correcting those who are in opposition (2 Timothy 2:22-25).

- Submit therefore to God. Resist the devil and he will flee from you. Draw near to God and He will draw near to you. Cleanse your hands, you sinners; and purify your hearts, you double-minded...Humble yourselves in the presence of the Lord, and He will exalt you.

  He who speaks against a brother or judges his brother, speaks against the law and judges the law; but if you judge the law, you are not a doer of the law but a judge of it. There is only one Lawgiver and Judge, the One who is able to save and to destroy; but who are you who judge your neighbor? (James 4:7-8, 10-12).

- In this you greatly rejoice, even though now for a little while, if necessary, you have been distressed by various trials, so that the proof of your faith, being more precious than gold which is perishable, even though tested by fire, may be found to result in praise and glory and honor at the revelation of Jesus Christ; and though you have not seen Him, you love Him, and though you do not see Him now, but believe in Him, you greatly rejoice with joy inexpressible and full of glory, obtaining as the outcome of your faith the salvation of your souls (1 Peter 1:6-9).

- Prepare your minds for action, keep sober in spirit, fix your hope completely on the grace to be brought to you at the revelation of Jesus Christ. As obedient children, do not be conformed to the former lusts which were yours in your ignorance, but like the Holy One who called you, be holy yourselves also in all your behavior; because it is written, "YOU SHALL BE HOLY FOR I AM HOLY" (1 Peter 1:13-16).

- Do not be surprised at the fiery ordeal among you, which comes upon you for your testing, as though some strange thing were happening to you; but to the degree that you share the sufferings of Christ, keep on rejoicing, so that also at the revelation of His glory you may rejoice with exultation. If you are reviled for the name of Christ, you are blessed, because the Spirit of glory and of God rests on you...If anyone suffers as a Christian, he is not to be ashamed, but is to glorify God in this name...Those also who suffer according to the will of God shall entrust their souls to a faithful Creator in doing what is right (1 Peter 4:12-14,16,19).

• Be of sober spirit, be on the alert. Your adversary, the devil, prowls around like a roaring lion, seeking someone to devour. But resist him, firm in your faith, knowing that the same experiences of suffering are being accomplished by your brethren who are in the world. After you have suffered for a little while, the God of all grace, who called you to His eternal glory in Christ, will Himself perfect, confirm, strengthen and establish you (1 Peter 5:8-10).

• False prophets also arose among the people, just as there will also be false teachers among you, who will secretly introduce destructive heresies, even denying the Master who bought them, bringing swift destruction upon themselves. Many will follow their sensuality, and because of them the way of the truth will be maligned; and in their greed they will exploit you with false words; their judgment from long ago is not idle, and their destruction is not asleep. For if God did not spare angels when they sinned, but cast them into hell and committed them to pits of darkness, reserved for judgment; and did not spare the ancient world, but preserved Noah, a preacher of righteousness, with seven others, when He brought a flood upon the world of the ungodly; and if He condemned the cities of Sodom and Gomorrah to destruction by reducing them to ashes, having made them an example to those who would live ungodly lives thereafter; and if He rescued righteous Lot, oppressed by the sensual conduct of unprincipled men (for by what he saw and heard that righteous man, while living among them, felt his righteous soul tormented day after day by their lawless deeds), then the Lord knows how to rescue the godly from temptation (2 Peter 2:1-9).

- Contend earnestly for the faith which was once for all handed down to the saints (Jude 3).

- You, beloved, ought to remember the words that were spoken beforehand by the apostles of our Lord Jesus Christ, that they were saying to you, "In the last time there will be mockers, following after their own ungodly lusts." These are the ones who cause divisions, worldly-minded, devoid of the Spirit. But you, beloved, building yourselves up on your most holy faith, praying in the Holy Spirit, keep yourselves in the love of God, waiting anxiously for the mercy of our Lord Jesus Christ to eternal life (Jude 17-21).

- And there was war in heaven, Michael and his angels waging war with the dragon. The dragon and his angels waged war, and they were not strong enough, and there was no longer a place found for them in heaven. And the great dragon was thrown down, the serpent of old who is called the devil and Satan, who deceives the whole world; he was thrown down to the earth, and his angels were thrown down with him. Then I heard a loud voice in heaven, saying, "Now the salvation, and the power, and the kingdom of our God and the authority of His Christ have come, for the accuser of our brethren has been thrown down, he who accuses them before our God day and night. And they overcame him because of the blood of the Lamb and because of the word of their testimony, and they did not love their life even when faced with death. For this reason, rejoice, O heavens and you who dwell in them" (Revelation 12:7-12).

Notes

Chapter 1—Know How to Fight

1. Stefan Verstappen, "Ancient Chinese Strategies Can Bring Victory in the Sparring Ring," *Black Belt* magazine, January 2000. Used by permission.

2. Tom Chiarella, "The Fistfight: A Primer," *Esquire*, May 15, 2007.

Chapter 2—Fight or Flight?

1. As taught by Kevin Hogan in *Covert Hypnosis* (Eagan, MN: Network 3000 Publishing, 2006).

2. Elisha A. Hoffman, "Leaning on the Everlasting Arms," *The Glad Evangel for Revival, Camp, and Evangelistic Meetings* (Dalton, GA: A.J. Showalter & Co., 1887).

3. Reb Bradley, "Exposing the Schemes of the Devil" in the Spiritual Warfare Series, Family Ministries © 1998, http://www.familyministries.com/schemes .html.

Chapter 3—Breakdown for a Blessing

1. "What Are Demons?" © 2006 Revelation of Truth Ministries, http://revelation oftruthministries.ca. Used by permission.

2. Adapted from a list compiled by Pastor Chris Simpson, © 1993–2005 by New Wine Christian Fellowship, Pasadena, TX.

3. Frank and Ida Mae Hammond, *Pigs in the Parlor: A Practical Guide to Deliverance* (Kirkwood, MO: Impact Books, 1973), 142.

Chapter 4—Weeds in the Garden

1. Ed Murphy, *The Handbook for Spiritual Warfare*, rev. and updated (Nashville: Thomas Nelson, 2003), 13.

Chapter 5—Rituals Untold

1. Charles Austin Miles, "In the Garden," 1912.

2. Frederick Whitfield, "Oh How I Love Jesus," 1855, in Whitfield, *Sacred Poems and Prose*, 1861.

3. Frank and Ida Mae Hammond, *Pigs in the Parlor: A Practical Guide to Deliverance* (Kirkwood, MO: Impact Books, 1973), 111-115.

Chapter 6—The Dynamic Duo

1. Wikipedia, s.v. "Holy Spirit," http://en.wikipedia.org/wiki/Holy_Spirit.

2. Loida Grant, "Christian Life Study Outlines: #5 The Holy Spirit," © 2007, from L.D.G. Ministry, www.ldgministry.org.

Chapter 9—Fixing Our Hair

1. Helen H. Lemmel, "Turn Your Eyes upon Jesus," *Glad Song*, 1922, public domain.

Chapter 11—Tightening Our Girdles

1. Adapted from scriptures compiled by Elwin and Margit Roach and presented on their "The Pathfinder" website: www.godfire.net. Used by permission.

Chapter 12—Putting on Our Stomping Shoes

1. Charlotte Elliott, "Just as I Am," 1835.

About the Author

Thelma Wells' life has been a courageous journey of faith. When she was born to an unwed teenager, the name on her birth certificate read simply "Baby Girl Morris." Her mother struggled to make ends meet by working as a maid in the "big house" while they lived in the servants' quarters.

When Thelma stayed at her grandparents' home, her grandmother locked her in a dark, smelly, insect-infested closet all day. In spite of her fear, Thelma sang every hymn and praise song she could remember. The Lord received her innocent praise and rewarded it with an abundant life of joy, protecting her from anger and bitterness.

A trailblazer for black women in many areas, Thelma worked in the banking industry and was a professor at Master's International School of Divinity. Her vivacious personality and talent for storytelling eventually pulled her into public ministry. Attracting the attention of the Women of Faith Tour, she was soon one of their core speakers. She was named Extraordinary Woman of the Year in 2008 by the Extraordinary Women Conferences.

Along with writing books, including *God Is Not Through with Me Yet*, Thelma is president of Woman of God Ministries. "Mama T," as she is affectionately called, helps girls and women all over the world discover Jesus and live for Him.

Thelma earned a bachelor's degree at North Texas State University and a master's of ministry from Master's International School of Divinity in Indiana. She was awarded an honorary doctorate from St. Thomas Christian College and Theological Seminary and ordained through the Association of Christian Churches in Florida

Thelma and George, her husband of 47 years and her best friend, supporter, and encourager, live in Texas and enjoy spending time with their three children, eight grandchildren, and three great-grandchildren.

Woman of God Ministries

Thelma founded Woman of God Ministries in 1994. The ministry's vision is to "cause effective, positive change in the people we serve, their families and their communities, by motivating and encouraging them to be their best for God."

She wants to teach and preach God's Word and principles and be a positive example to girls and women (Titus 2:3-5 and Proverbs 31). Her vision is to see people healed, saved, and delivered by God's grace and then be empowered by the Holy Spirit to do the work for which God has called them.

Woman of God Ministries lifts up the name of Jesus Christ and provides a safe place for those who have been wounded by the world so that they can be saved, healed, set free, and matured in Christ. With "In Christ, you can BEE the best!" (Philippians 4:13) as a motto, Thelma's organization says…

By God's help we can:
Bee aware of who we are
Eliminate the negatives
Strive for Eternal value
Have overwhelming Success!
B+E+E=S

For more information about Thelma's ministry,
please check out her website:
www.ThelmaWells.com